How to Deal with How You Feel

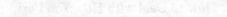

How to Deal with
How You Feel

Ralph Speas

BROADMAN PRESS
Nashville, Tennessee

© Copyright 1980 • Broadman Press

4252-78

ISBN: 0-8054-5278-8

Dewey Decimal Classification: 152.4

Subject heading: EMOTIONS

Library of Congress Catalog Card Number: 80-65316

Printed in the United States of America

To the one whose life
exhibits superbly what I teach,
my wife, Rosene,
I affectionately dedicate this volume.

Foreword

Where does a person go for answers? It is amazing where we seek advice. We go to the one who has failed, "who has been there." He can empathize, but can a failure give good counsel? We try the "professional" even if he is of a different persuasion philosophically and spiritually. Where should we go? The One who is perfect, successful, and all-wise, cannot be a bad choice and His answers are found in the ageless book, the Bible.

When did biblical Christianity quit supplying answers for the psychological needs of humanity? Are pastors unnecessarily referring some individuals to others whose specialty is to treat emotional problems? Increasingly, I am discovering that we have somehow come to believe that real help is available *only* outside the church, outside the pastor's office, outside the Bible.

As a Bible teacher and pastor, I found myself flooded with counselees trying to find ways to resolve their problems. There I was in a dilemma. Either I could send these people for professional help fifty miles away or help them myself. Most couldn't afford the expense or the time for weekly trips so far away. I was forced to do the job, and relied heavily on the Holy Spirit to guide me to answers. One good result was my intensive search in the

Word, which brought me personal happiness and also gave me competence as I shared with problem-ridden counselees.

For a period of time I resigned my pastorate to take on a full-time practice as counselor. Now, I'm not a psychologist and have never pretended to be one. However, my schedule has been full of appointments with those desiring psychological assistance. Many of those who came had previously spent years receiving therapy. Among those who came for scriptural guidance was a psychiatrist. I found the timeless principles of God's Word life-changing.

Perhaps life is faster nowadays. Man had problems with emotions when the pace was not as maddening. But it is my opinion that our lifestyle today has pushed us, intensifying our emotions, causing unusual stress and strain man has seldom known in days past. If this is true, it's also true that God's grace is sufficient regardless of the unique pressures of our society. One translation of Paul's statement in Romans 12:2 appropriately enjoins, "Don't let the world around you squeeze you into its own mold" (Phillips).

This morning as we had family devotions a number of people began to parade through my mind as we prayed. I thought of the man I saw yesterday who has lived in years of mental torment. He has had over thirty shock treatments and has existed on only the most powerful tranquilizers. God, through his Word, is communicating to him and he's changing. He wants to show his psychiatrist the Bible studies that have helped him and wants to recommend these to all his fellow patients! Last night a lady called about a suicidal friend who is desperate for help. Also last evening, a lady called about her brother who has threatened to kill his family. My heart goes out to a young father I saw yesterday whose wife left him for a life of immorality. He's brokenhearted but said, "God is helping me." All these are trying to deal with how they feel.

When trying to create a title for this volume, I was hoping to project the book's message. *How To Deal With How You Feel* helped, but it didn't capsulize all I wished it could say. However, a stanza from Fannie Crosby's song "Rescue the Perishing" just about says it all:

> Down in the human heart, Crushed by the tempter,
> Feelings lie buried that grace can restore;
> Touched by a loving heart, Wakened by kindness,
> Chords that are broken will vibrate once more.

Contents

1
"Why Art Thou Cast Down, O My Soul?" (Ps. 42:5)

A college student, she was brilliant and a leader. Her charm and pleasant manner won her popularity on campus. Then her sister died of cancer. It seemed to be an untimely death. Within two years her father was struck down in middle age by a fatal heart attack. Her grief and loneliness were almost more than she could bear. When she seemed to be hurting most, she received the tragic word that her brother had committed suicide.

Moods of depression became all too frequent. Her chemistry was badly shaken. She was diagnosed as hypoglycemic and allergic to a long list of foods. She could identify with the psalmist. "Why art thou cast down, O my soul? and why art thou disquieted in me?" Was there an answer? Physicians could not help her. The usual medication prescribed to calm, to perk up, to make tranquil only disturbed her body chemistry the more. Then, one day I received a letter from this lovely girl. She had found her answers in Christ. When all failed, she discovered "the Spirit also helpeth our infirmities" (Rom. 8:26).

While it's true that Christ is the answer and that the Spirit of God helps us in our infirmities, there are still many Christians who wrestle every day with debilitating emotions.

A beautiful couple fell in love and married. He was extremely ambitious, and she was a perfectionist. He enjoyed people, and his call to the ministry gave him great satisfaction. Perhaps his unbounded joy and total delight with his work as pastor made her somewhat jealous. People came to Christ through his ministry and the church grew. She was seldom noticed. Her husband got all the attention. Didn't people understand that behind every great man was a great woman? She always gave constructive criticism, and her husband welcomed it. He valued her advice and believed this was a great contribution to his success. But the tap, tap, tapping of her "constructive" criticism was obviously void of praise and encouragement. The 95 percent that was right went unnoticed. The 5 percent he did wrong was always pointed out. It began to eat at him, and his quiet moods at home made his wife suspicious. She accused him one day of having a lover. This broke his heart. As a man of God he had avoided infidelity, and his heart had always been set on being faithful. To him, the wife was becoming a nag and a hag. She no longer looked beautiful. The obvious lack of communication began to trouble the wife. She began to see herself as a critic and tried to correct herself. But it had gone too far. He resented his wife deeply, but swallowed the bitterness and plodded on as minister and friend of the people. The work was now getting to him. He was burned out on visitation. Sermon preparation was neglected. The deacons irritated him, and he wondered if he should resign. A different setting, he thought, might bring back his motivation and zeal. Sometimes he wished he was not married. Divorce was out of the question. He would never admit that occasionally he wondered how it would be if his wife died.

The resentment deepened, and depression was more frequent. His wife made every effort to love him, to praise him, to encourage him. Sometimes he wished to be sick; perhaps that would make her feel bad. He hoped she was aware that she had driven him to uselessness and failure. Now, he was in a trap. He wanted revenge, but he also wanted to be released from his bitterness. He hoped the torment he was causing his wife would pay her back. But the debt she owed was too great, and his whole life was consumed with making her pay.

The deacons approached their minister and secretly insisted on his resignation. He'd lost his place of service. He hoped his wife knew she was to blame.

He was a man broken by bitterness. Resentment had made him a slave. Is there a way out of such a dilemma? Is there an answer? "Create in me a clean heart, O God; and renew a right spirit within me" (Ps. 51:10).

As a young pastor, I sat in my office discouraged with my failure to help people. I thought of my physician friend, a specialist in internal medicine, who treated as many as fifty people a day, competently writing prescriptions, advising surgery, bed rest, and other treatments. However, he had patients with sicknesses that were emotionally induced and sent some of these people my way. I was the soul specialist, after all, and should be able to care for these as competently as he ministered to the organically ill.

One such patient poured out his story to me. He had

lost forty pounds. It all began when the person he loved *and* abused the most walked out of his life. She had been married to him long enough. I didn't help that man, nor did I give relief to the desperate alcoholic the doctor sent my way.

I prayed, "Lord, I'm a minister of the gospel. I'm supposed to help these people. I need answers. Aren't there solutions to the problems of these troubled souls? God help me." It was then that the Lord directed me to Colossians 2:10, "And ye are complete in him." The Lord spoke to me as clearly as if he had said it out loud, "Ralph, your competence is in me." From that day I've looked to Jesus for the answers. To my amazement the answers began to come from his Word! People have been helped as I stood back and watched the power of his Word operate in their lives.

What a joy it has been to discover the full implications of receiving Christ as Lord and Savior! Paul said, "As ye have therefore received Christ Jesus the Lord, so walk ye in him" (Col. 2:6). Receiving Jesus is only the beginning. As the fullness of God was in him, so when we receive him we begin to receive the fullness and peace of God.

For several years in my private counseling practice, I have always explained to those who come for help my firm belief that the Bible has the answers. God has sent my way the educated and uneducated, professors and students, physicians and the physically sick, psychiatrists and psychotics, skeptics and "saints," businessmen and laborers, and in each case I have determined to help them on the basis of biblical wisdom. It has worked! But there is a catch. It has worked with those who will submit themselves to the authority of God's Word.

Naturally, the first step to wholeness is developing a personal relationship with Jesus, the Word, the One whose words are spirit and life.[1] Jesus came for the purpose of bringing life—*abundant life* to his followers. The impression that the world gets from many Christians is that being a Christian is a living death. They don't want any part of it. Who can blame them? The way you deal with how you feel is not just a private concern of yours. It's a Kingdom matter. How you handle your feelings has effects far beyond what you imagine. God cares how you feel. He has given you His Word and His Spirit. The purpose of the following chapters is to share with you scriptural directions on how you can work together with God in dealing with how you feel.

Note

1. See Appendix A for detailed instructions on how to develop a personal relationship with God through Jesus Christ.

2
Emotions, Our Friends

I found myself unusually depressed. Having lost motivation to work, I rationalized that I deserved a time of rest. I felt miserable in my despondent mood, and it occurred to me that there must be a reason for this depression. Going back in my mind a few days, I recognized three unresolved problem areas which were greatly troubling me. I realized I had put off doing something important, and this was bothering me. Second, I was troubled about how to accomplish a pressing project. There was no way to move ahead without some answers. Third, I was anxious about something totally out of my control. I thought there was nothing I could do to correct the situation.

The Lord talked to me that day. I was convicted about putting off what had to be done, and I immediately took care of it. The Lord assured me that answers would come in his time regarding the pressing project if I'd simply trust him. And the situation out of my hands should obviously be left for God to work out.

The cause of my depression was rooted in my procrastination and lack of total dependence on God. Depression was an indication or a symptom of two bad characteristics in my life-style.

Emotions are our friends, often telling us that certain

issues need to be resolved; attitudes need to be changed; relationships need to be corrected. Just as a fever or high white cell count indicates an infection, an emotion can be symptomatic of an underlying problem, too.

Vernon Grounds once said, "Psychic pain is inflicted by the Holy Spirit as He creates the conviction of sin, a conviction which testifies that God's law has been broken."[1] Guilt thus becomes our friend, because it tells us that we need to resolve the sin within. Fear may be telling us that we aren't properly trusting the Lord. Loneliness may be telling us that we count more on the friendship of others than on a friendship with God.

Then, there are the positive, light emotions that are the sunshine in our lives. While the lighter emotions such as joy and peace indicate life is rolling along quite well, they should never be so authoritative as to confirm one's spirituality. Indeed, a spiritual man may be void of emotion, and at times a man out of God's will may feel very happy for the moment. But for the most part a man whose life is yielded to Christ's control (as we shall see in later chapters) and whose life-style conforms to the Word is usually the man who most enjoys the lighter emotions.

Emotions not only serve as symptoms of spiritual-psychological problems, but they can be symptoms of physical disorders.

A lady sat across the table in my office. She was trembling. "I think I'm going to have a nervous breakdown," she said. After listening to her at length I recognized some unwarranted guilt and worked with her to get rid of it. The next day she phoned me in a worse state of mind and body. As we talked, it dawned on me that her problems began weeks before, following a big dinner out of town with friends. She had eaten breakfast just before calling me. It occurred to me that something she ate might have triggered her depression. I encouraged her to see a physician that same day. She was given some tests, and the results indicated an allergy to grain foods. The way she felt was symptomatic of a genuine physical problem.

From my counseling experiences through the years, however, I've discovered that emotional reactions, for the most part, do not arise from the physical but from the spiritual.

Basically, the soul has three parts. They are the intellect, will, and emotions. How we think (intellect) and act (will) determines how we will feel (emotions). A number of psychologists believe that feeling follows behavior.

If we want to correct how we feel, we need to correct what we think and how we behave. The Bible supplies numerous examples of this principle which we shall study in later chapters.

At this point in your reading, examine how you feel. Are you depressed, feeling guilty or resentful? Are you angry or overcome by fear, loneliness, or worry? Do you feel elated, joyful, peaceful, loving? Exactly what feeling is predominant in your life today?

Certain feelings have a tendency to control our lives. I often ask myself, "Who's in control of my life? The Lord or I?" One day while praying it occurred to me that it was easier to determine whether I was in control if I could detect a dominating emotion. I would ask myself, "Is fear in control of my life today? Anger? Guilt? Resentment? Loneliness? Grief? Worry? Desire?" So often, I realized that one of those emotions was actually coloring the events of my day and influencing my decisions.

Take time to confess the sin of letting an emotion control your life today, if that's the case. Apply his promise to forgive and cleanse you (1 John 1:9).

With Christ's help, dethrone the dominating emotion and ask him to occupy the position of control.

Note

1. Vernon Grounds, "When and Why the Psychiatrist Can't Help You," *Seminary Study Series* (Denver: Conservative Baptist Theological Seminary, n.d.), p. 3.

3
Dealing with Depression

Depression is a general feeling of unhappiness. There are many and various causes of the emotional states we label with the word *depression.* Depression is related to other emotions. What I shall say in subsequent chapters about other emotions will relate to depression. For that reason, the present chapter will be short and to the point.

Depression is sometimes related to physical causes. A hormone imbalance, wrong diet, lack of sleep, or physical trauma such as surgery can trigger depression. I've known of cases in which depression set in after eating certain foods. For this reason I always ask depressed persons to see a physician for a physical examination if there are no obvious spiritual or emotional causes for their depression.

For the most part, however, I find much depression is an emotional tiredness or fatigue. Just as an individual becomes physically tired after exerting himself physically, the same person can find himself emotionally exhausted or depressed after exerting himself emotionally.

If an individual expends a great deal of guilt energy, he'll become depressed. In the Bible, King David (Ps. 38:4) indicated that his iniquities caused his depressed

state. King Saul repeatedly went into depression following his acts of disobedience (1 Sam. 13:11-13; 15:7-11,
17-24). When Elijah was fear-ridden, he slipped into
deep depression (1 Kings 19:1-18).

Depression can be caused by anger, anxiety, resentment, loneliness, grief, and fear. If you can trace your
depression back to a negative emotion and isolate the
emotion you can usually deal with it successfully.

Tim LaHaye, in his book, *How to Win Over Depression*, says he discovered an element always present in
depression: self-pity. Depression, he says, equals *trauma*
plus self-pity.[1]

There is no question about it. A depressed person feels
very sorry for himself and is extremely self-oriented.

I always attempt to take a person back to the traumas
that resulted in his negative emotion. For instance, I take
the person back to

. . . his sin (trauma) that resulted in guilt, or

. . . the offense by someone (trauma) resulting in his bitterness, or

. . . the violation of a right (trauma) provoking his
anger, or

. . . the vexing situation (trauma) that caused the
anxiety, or

. . . the frightening situation (trauma) that resulted in
fear,

. . . the loss in death or separation (trauma) that gave rise
to grief, or

. . . the aloneness (trauma) that developed into loneliness.

Self-pity added to any trauma and its resultant emotion results in a growing depression. Emotionally de-

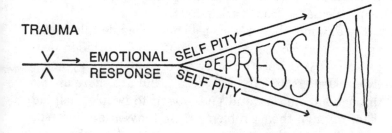

pressed people always feel sorry for themselves. Tragic-
ally, the more a person feels sorry for himself the greater
the depression grows.

If individuals are to avoid nearly irreparable damage
from depression, the fondling of self must cease. I'm sure
Job experienced depression, and it seemed that nothing
could change his circumstances. But everything
changed; even heaven moved on his behalf when he
began to think compassionately about others. "And the
Lord turned the captivity of Job when he prayed for his
friends: also the Lord gave Job twice as much as he had
before" (Job 42:10). Somehow everything changes, even
our depression, when we start doing for others and stop
dwelling on ourselves.

My wife tells me that her depression is usually broken
by two responses. First, she begins to thank God for the

blessings in her life, and then she tries to think of something to do for someone else.

As much as I may not feel like it, I find worshiping God by singing songs of thanksgiving and praise often helps release me from dark moods.

My day may begin with a heavy schedule filled with appointments to see depressed and problem-ridden people. My first temptation may be to view that day negatively. Depression can easily result. But as I share myself throughout the day and give myself to people, helping them through their problems, I find myself exhilarated, not exhausted. Yes, depression can be broken when self-pity is changed into service to others.

The Way Out

1. *Trace depression to the time it started.* This often helps to isolate the problem. It may help to ask yourself what emotions are or have been occupying your time. Look at the major or most frequent dark emotions, such as resentment, guilt, fear, worry, and anger. After the emotion or emotions are isolated, determine what trauma precipitated the emotion (such as the sin that resulted in guilt, or the offense that resulted in anger or bitterness).

2. *Confess all unforgiven sins.* Our wrong responses to life situations are clearly sin. A negative reaction to an offense is sin. A negative reaction to aloneness is sin. A negative reaction to a frightening situation is sin. A negative reaction to a vexing situation is sin. The admission that the reaction was wrong is extremely therapeutic. It is the path to the cleansing of an attitude.

3. *Correct your responses.* Instead of wallowing in self, begin to pray for your friends, or in some way do something good for others. Confession is the correct response to guilt. Enjoy God's cleansing and forgive yourself. Instead of being resentful, begin to forgive. Instead of living in fear, begin to accomplish labors of love and depend on God to supply strength and courage needed. Instead of exploding over an injustice begin to thank God for the privilege of life. Instead of grieving over your aloneness, take advantage of your solitary moments by communing with the Lord and occupying your time with constructive activities.

Take Positive Action Now

The temptation is to let the depression "blow over." To yield to it is a serious mistake and only leads to more depression in the future.

Even if you don't feel like taking any positive steps toward resolving your depression, you will find wholeness sooner if you take action now—regardless of how "down" you feel.

Depression is unquestionably a great deterrent to doing the will of God. One of the most valuable lessons a person can learn is that obedience in doing what God requires is more important than how one feels. To let depression keep us from accomplishing his will when we have the physical ability and spiritual power available to overcome it is to make depression our master and lord.

Elijah was deeply depressed. Wallowing in self-pity, he thought he was the only one serving God. His wrong responses to the spiritual decadence of the day and to

Jezebel's threat on his life were fear and self-pity. Two events helped turn the tide for him, and both were initiated by the Lord. In the first place, the Lord gave him nutritious food and some undisturbed sleep. Second, the Lord spoke to Elijah with his still small voice (1 Kings 19:1-18).

Friend, take time to let God speak to you; eat a good meal with some loved one; begin to take the three steps out of your depression; and get a good night's sleep.

Note

1. Tim LaHaye, *How To Win Over Depression* (Grand Rapids, Michigan: Zondervan, 1974).

4
The Secret to Stability

I've discovered something in every person I've known who has experienced emotional difficulties: the refusal or the inability to accept something in life. It usually begins with the refusal to accept, followed by the inability.

Alan had a history of emotional sickness. He spent several months in a mental hospital and received years of psychiatric therapy. When he came to my office he hadn't worked in three years. At home he read his favorite sports magazines all night and slept all day. It was obvious he felt guilty that his wife supported him and his son. Daytime meant responsibility. That's when he slept. When everyone was sleeping he wasn't faced with responsibility, and that's when he felt most comfortable awake. It became apparent to me that this man was playing a game. His stay in the hospital was an obvious retreat from responsibility. His daytime sleeping habits indicated the same. His refusal to accept responsibility precipitated most of his emotional problems. Anxiety, depression, and worry took up the greatest share of his emotional energy, all because he refused to accept something.

A middle-aged man told me how much he disliked his looks, his abilities, his parents, and his past life of poverty. Harold refused to accept himself as God had made him. When I visited him in the hospital months later he was barely recognizable. He actually looked twenty-five years older than he was. His great loss of weight was the result of depression. I had never seen this happen before, but I saw that man languish into an irretrievable state. Weeks later he died, refusing to accept himself as God made him.

Lydia was a brilliant young lady holding a professorship in a large university. I gasped as she stepped into my office. Normally she weighed 125 pounds, but there she stood, an ugly skeleton of skin and bones weighing about eighty pounds. She, too, could not accept herself. Suffering from *anorexia nervosa*, she hated the idea of being fat. She had no fear of death, but had an inordinate fear of fat—not understanding God created adipose tissue for very good reasons.

In the considerable time since I had held her mother's funeral, Sharon hadn't been to church. I stopped by to see her and her husband one afternoon. There she sat on the couch in a fetal position with a blanket wrapped around her. At times such as this she would regress to childhood, sit in a corner, and cry. Her problem? She refused to accept her mother's death. I tried sharing with her the need to overcome her grief and giving her some sound scriptural advice, but she refused to cooperate. I saw her in a psychiatric ward months later with a new grief. Her husband had left her, and no matter what she did to try and retrieve her losses she couldn't. She still refused to accept the death of her mother.

If you study past moments of depression and emotional turmoil, you, too, will probably find yourself putting your finger on something you refused to accept.

I've found that those things which we refuse to accept in life can easily be listed under one of five categories. Let's look at each of these separately.

Refusal to Accept God-Given Roles

An individual who refuses to accept certain roles in life will eventually face frustration and emotional turmoil. His problem is simple. Anxiety, guilt, fear, and anger often surface. Secular psychology such as Reality Therapy has had amazing success with prison inmates by helping them define responsibility and holding them accountable for responsible behavior.

The wife who struggles with her role as mate and mother, refusing to accept the responsibilities attached, often lives with anxiety, anger, and depression. The husband who spends an inordinate amount of time and energy on his career or personal recreation is apt to carry a load of guilt.

Individuals who ignore moral responsibilities try to do away with the source of morality by calling themselves atheists. From my own experience, it seems to me that the most depressed, the most emotionally distressed people are those who struggle with the guilt that accompanies acts of disobedience, and sexual immorality in particular.

The father who refuses to accept his roles and responsibilities begins to reap certain consequences that he cannot handle. Frustration becomes complicated by his guilt.

Irresponsibility is an enemy to happiness. The only way out is to accept responsibility and the roles God has given and press on by faith in the strength Christ gives.

One young father hated work and quit. He couldn't justify his irresponsibility. In his deep depression he was hospitalized and eventually institutionalized. He was safe in these places. (Some psychologists believe that most people who frequent the psychiatric wards want to. It's one way to escape responsibility.) To help this father adjust to life, I tried to find out how much responsibility he would accept as husband and parent. On a scale of 0 to 100 he finally said he could accept 30 percent. Looking at him, I said, "As a Christian, you could have indicated 100 percent. The Bible says you can do anything God asks you to do with the help and strength Christ gives" (Phil. 4:13).

The secret to stability is acceptance, the acceptance of roles and responsibilities, realizing that "faithful is he that called you who also will do it" (1 Thess. 5:14).

Refusal to Accept Authority

An individual who refuses to accept authority will develop emotional problems. The problem defined: insubordination.

A driver who always breaks the speed limit experiences a special tension. He tries to reduce the tension by buying a CB or a "fuzz-buster" to detect radar devices. What a price for insubordination!

Teenagers often register irritation because they are

constantly pushing the limit of authority. Testing authority at school, home, and church means living with a special kind of turmoil.

Paranoia and fear reside in the heart of the violator. "The wicked flee when no man pursueth" (Prov. 28:1). The refusal to accept authority does have its emotional consequences.

The disobedient child, the uncooperative wife, the insubordinate employee, and the criminal have one thing in common: the refusal to accept authority. Proof that insubordination causes emotional problems is seen in our prisons. Perhaps the greatest incidence of neuroses and psychoses is seen in penal institutions.

Submission to authority is a key principle to social harmony and peace. In the epistles, the writers repeatedly admonish us to cooperate with the authority over us, knowing that such authority is God-ordained (Rom. 13:1-4) for our own good. Very seldom do we think of emotional wholeness in relationship to this great principle.

Rebellion is the same as insubordination, and in every case of rebellion you can see the torment of frustrated emotions.

Refusal to Accept One's God-Given Self

A person's refusal to accept himself as God made him can be accompanied by a variety of emotional problems. Everyone struggles with this issue sometime in life. For some people, self-concept problems surface all through life. Some never have a healthy self-image, while others learn self-acceptance by adulthood.

Some of the most depressed people I've been around are those who refuse to accept themselves. Feelings of inferiority seem insurmountable.

One young lady expressed a real dislike for herself when she described her bitterness about being single. She always felt her sister enjoyed the limelight, praise, and breaks in life. She detested her own appearance and lack of ability. One of the issues that often surfaced in our conversations was her salvation. God didn't like her because he didn't do a good job making her, she thought. If she couldn't trust God for the way he made her, she thought, how could she trust God for her eternal destiny?

It was difficult for her to accept the fact that God had designed her uniquely for a special purpose. She needed to be able to say, with the Psalmist: "I will praise thee; for I am fearfully and wonderfully made" (Ps. 139:14). No matter how we compare ourselves with others, we must realize that an omniscient God made us like we are for a special reason. We have no right to dispute with God concerning his design. "Woe unto him that striveth with his Maker!" (Isa. 45:9).

The first step to self-acceptance is the acceptance of God's design for life. Refusal to accept what God designed and produced only results in frustration, negativism, and unhappiness.

A teenager once remarked to me that he hated his body. He wished he could have his brother's body. His refusal to accept himself as God made him threw him into a state of depression and self-preoccupation that made his life most miserable. A young man now, he is brilliant, has an unusual ability with words, and is extremely artistic, but he remains useless and unproductive. He refuses to accept himself.

A little girl scrawled on a home-made plaque, "I'm me and I'm wonderful 'cause God don't make no junk."

Refusal to Accept Others

Intolerance for others only results in misery and frustration. The refusal to accept others was of great concern to our Lord, and he clearly stated our responsibility to love. It is not only good for others, it is equally good for us.

We try to change everyone around us to our liking, when our time should be spent changing ourselves. It is obvious I can't change the world, but I can change myself.

Love is the acceptance of people where they are. We certainly can't condone their sinful actions, but we can accept the sinner.

Husbands try to change their wives, when their responsibility is to love them. Wives try to change their husbands, not realizing that the home is more peaceful and satisfying when they simply love.

Intolerance for others is usually detected in our disdain, resentment, jealousy, and hatred. We find ourselves vindictive, argumentative, critical, and rude.

Refusal to Accept Life

The refusal to accept life as it comes our way is an indication that we clearly misunderstand God's basic intentions for us. Joseph's plight in Egypt with all its adversities and reverses seemed bad, but in retrospect he said, "God meant it unto good, to bring to pass, as it is this day, to save much people" (Gen. 50:20). "For I know the thoughts that I think toward you, saith the Lord, thoughts of peace, and not of evil, to give you an expected end" (Jer. 29:11).

The Christian should be able to say with the apostle Paul, "And we know that all things work together for good to them that love God, to them who are the called according to his purpose" (Rom. 8:28).

For these reasons we should be able to accept the good with the bad in life, and we can register this acceptance through thanksgiving. God led Habakkuk the prophet to a high level of mature contentment. This unique statement shows Habakkuk's adjustment to the adversities of life: "Although the fig tree shall not blossom, neither shall fruit be in the vines; the labour of the olive shall fail, and fields shall yield no meat; the flock shall be cut off from the fold and there shall be no herd in the stalls: Yet I will rejoice in the Lord, I will joy in the God of my salvation" (Hab. 3:17-18).

Now we know the secret to Paul's contentment in life. "I have learned," he said, "in whatsoever state I am, therewith to be content. I know both how to be abased, and I know how to abound: every where and in all things I am instructed both to be full and to be hungry, both to abound and to suffer need" (Phil. 4:11-12). Do you note that spirit of acceptance? No matter whether life was easy or difficult, he accepted it with thanksgiving. This is why he said, "In every thing give thanks: for this is the will of God in Christ Jesus concerning you" (1 Thess. 5:18).

The secret to stability is acceptance. We must learn to

accept our roles, authority, ourselves, other people, and life as it comes.

If I refuse to accept my roles I become *irresponsible.* If I refuse to accept authority I become *insubordinate.* If I do not accept myself I feel *inferior.* If I don't accept people I'm *intolerant.* If I don't accept life as it comes my way, I register my *ingratitude.* Do you suffer from irresponsibility, insubordination, inferiority, intolerance, or ingratitude? If you do, there's a way out.

Begin by praying this classic prayer: "Lord, grant me the serenity to accept the things I cannot change, the courage to change what I can and the wisdom to know the difference."

5
Relief from Resentment

Resentment is a deceptive emotion. Most people do not understand how powerful and life-changing it can be. I've seen personalities totally altered by it. It has been the defeat of many promising individuals. People have died premature deaths because of its silent presence, and others have spent thousands of dollars in hospitals trying to cure the physical maladies for which resentment was responsible.

What puzzles me is that some people will admit bitterness but not feel any urgency to alleviate it. A few actually seem to enjoy holding a grudge. They are determined to make someone pay.

Let's take a closer look at resentment. I find that resentment, often referred to as bitterness or a grudge, is a mixture of hate and hurt. Having been offended, let down, or deceived, the person is hurt. His response to the wound leaves him bitter or better. Not everyone responds negatively to a hurt. But those who do, plant the seed of resentment. Once it begins to grow its effects are devastating.

I know of no emotion as damaging as resentment. It actually alters appearance, causes depression, and consumes what could have been beautiful hours of relaxation. If there is one good thing about resentment, it has yet to be discovered.

Resentment Damages Relationships

In Hebrews 12:15, three things are discovered about bitterness or resentment. In the first place, *it grows.* "Lest any root of bitterness springing up trouble you, and thereby many be defiled." Notice words such as "root" and "springing up." Resentment, unlike grief or sorrow, does not die; it grows. Like Bermuda grass, it can look dead in the winter, but when the heat is on it spreads. Resentment may seem dormant or dead, but when the heat is on it grows. It doesn't take much to reveal its existence.

Second, *resentment causes trouble.* "Lest any root of bitterness . . . trouble you." The word for trouble has reference to a crowd of people. Bitterness always disturbs others, and a bitter person seldom makes a good impression on others. Indeed, he becomes a source of irritation. He's heard in the Sunday School class, on committees, in fellowships, and is always a problem.

Third, *resentment defiles:* "Thereby many be defiled." Unfortunately, resentment defiles the good thinking of others, and a resentful person discourages those around him. He is not satisfied to keep his bitterness to himself. He contaminates his family and friends.

As you can see, bitterness damages relationships. It causes friction and conflict. People hate to be around us with our negative attitudes, and those who have to put up with our resentment may very well take on that resentment. Thus, we sow "discord among brethren" (Prov. 6:19).

Resentment Deteriorates the Personality

When a person resents, he doesn't think positively about others. He thinks negatively. Philippians 4:8 says we ought to think on things in others that are true, honest, just, pure, lovely, of good report, and praiseworthy. But a resentful person can only see the dishonesty, the unfairness, the impurity, the ugliness, and the worst in the person he resents. Negative thinking is in direct violation of God's plan for abundant living.

What's frightening is the tendency a person has to become exactly like the bad in the individual he resents. Solomon said, "For as he thinketh in his heart, so is he" (Prov. 23:7). If all you think about is the bad in someone else, your thinking will begin to reflect that bad quality in your life-style. You may never look like the one you resent, but you'll display his greed, his selfishness, his dishonesty. Not only do psychologists agree on this, but the Bible definitely teaches this to be the case. You'll become exactly in personality like the bad in the personality you resent. Just give it time!

Wayne was a wife-beater and alcoholic. In an interview I discovered hostility toward his father. He hated his dad. The bitterness backfired on him. His dad was a wife-beater and alcoholic, too. As a teenager he would throw himself between his violent father and innocent mother. He would weep before his father and beg him to stop drinking. Wayne's bitterness catapulted him into a life-style just like his father's.

There's one more fact about personality deterioration. 1 John 2:9 shows that my insistence on holding a grudge against someone puts out the light of creativity: "He that saith he is in the light, and hateth his brother, is in darkness even until now." The Greeks believed light symbolized wisdom, knowledge, discretion, and imagination. John indicates that an individual who hates is incapable of good wisdom, discretion, and imagination, and thus void of the ability to make good decisions. A person who resents will discover his ability to make wise decisions is crippled. Bitterness puts the mind out of focus and bad decisions result.

A wife announced to me one day that she was going to file for divorce. Obviously her heart was a hotbed of resentment. I asked her if with my help she would work on her resentment before making that decision. She consented. In the next two weeks I counselled with her. During this time she came to know Christ personally and experienced a release from her resentment. She then said to me, "I've changed my mind. I'm not going to divorce my husband." As long as she had resentment she couldn't make the right decision regarding her marriage.

Businessmen make mistakes with resentment. Executives make bad decisions with resentment. Parents whose minds are filled with resentment also make decisions they'll regret, and the children usually pay for it.

Resentment Damages Spiritual Vitality

You will notice in Ephesians 4 that bitterness is in the context of *grieving the Holy Spirit*. Like a dove that refuses to fight back, the Holy Spirit simply ceases to manifest his power in our lives when we resent. How many times can you pinpoint spiritual defeat to a time when you began to resent someone?

1 John 4:20 says our *love for God* is impaired when we

resent someone. Often we want to love God with all our mind, soul, strength, heart, and might. But we'll never be able to love him as we ought as long as bitterness fills our souls.

My heart aches for pastors whose influence and preaching are ineffective because they allow bitterness to occupy their hearts and time. Almost daily I see homes wrecked by resentment and children lost to the secular world because of bitter parents.

Do you have resentment? Before you read on, write down the names of persons you resent. Arrange them in the order of greatest resentment. Take time to evaluate just how resentment has damaged some of your relationships, deteriorated your personality, and destroyed spiritual vitality.

Resentment Destroys

We've already discovered from the Scriptures that resentment ruins friendships, damages personality, and destroys spiritual vitality. The Bible teaches that resentment grows, causes trouble, contaminates relationships, makes you think negatively, causes you to become like the one you resent, puts your thinking out of focus, impairs your love to God, grieves the Holy Spirit, and makes your mind a slave to the one you resent.

There Is Relief

A lady came to my office and expressed a genuine desire to clear up her bitterness. What she had to share went back a long time, and her resentment ran deep. I must confess I was doubtful whether I could help her, although I desired greatly to do everything possible to help her find relief. I shared with her the principles related in this chapter. She responded positively and did *everything* I asked her to do. Within a month there was a dramatic change in her life. Even her countenance took on a radiance and added beauty.

If you are bitter and want release, you too can find freedom if you'll follow these principles exactly. The plan will work if you work it. There are three steps to take in resolving resentment.

A Clear Conscience

A clear conscience is a conscience that can look at God or man and say, "There's nothing between you and me." This may require asking forgiveness or even making restitution.

If you don't have a clear conscience, the Bible indicates that you are on a destruction course in regard to your faith (1 Tim. 1:19-20). You will undergo, as a Christian, severe chastening, and you'll experience an inability to be discerning or make good decisions (Heb. 5:13-14).

Whenever we're resentful we usually offend in some way the party who makes us bitter. Usually our offenses are reactions to their actions which caused our bitterness. You'll never resolve your resentment until you clear up the wrong you've committed, whether it was retaliatory or not. Above all, our bitterness is sin and requires the forgiveness of God. Our consciences will never be clear until we confess our sin to God. Therefore, we discover that cleansing a conscience is vertical and horizontal. We must seek forgiveness from God and man (1 John 1:9; Matt. 7:4-5; Jas. 5:16).

Commitment

The second step to resolving resentment is commitment, commitment to forgive. Forgiveness involves the will.

I must *consciously* forgive: "forgiving one another, even as God for Christ's sake hath forgiven you" (Eph. 4:32). I won't wake up some morning to discover I am suddenly forgiving. No, forgiveness is a deliberate act of the will.

In order to affect the will I must develop a mental attitude of forgiveness. A forgiving attitude is the outcome of Bible study and an understanding of God's ways.

A young mother was having problems, and everything pointed to some hidden resentment she possessed. One day she finally admitted, "Yes, I have resentment! And I'll tell you why. My stepfather raped me when I was a teenager. Every time he holds my little girls I hate it. I have a right to be bitter, don't I?" "Yes," I answered, "you have a right to be bitter, but I must warn you that bitterness will eventually destroy you." Somehow what I said didn't convince her. I then shared with her how it was when Jesus was crucified. The artists are kind in their portrayal of our Lord. There's every indication that Jesus was stripped naked and publicly humiliated. His exposure was as degrading and offensive as this young mother's rape. I continued, "As Jesus was exposed and humiliated, do you know what he said? 'Father, forgive them; for they know not what they do.' When Jesus forgave he understood that those men did not know what they were doing. After your stepfather raped you he probably wondered why he did it and regrets to this day his terrible deed." Forgiveness realizes that the person who has hurt us does not always understand why he acted so offensively.

Forgiveness also understands that God permitted the situation whereby we were offended. In Romans 8:28, it is clear that the Lord controls the events of our lives, and suffering is not meant for evil but for good. In 1 Corinthians 10:13, we read that no trial that takes us is uncommon to man, and God will not permit us to be tried without providing a way of escape. He controls the trial so that as we respond to it properly it will turn out for our good. Forgiveness simply sees the person who hurts me as a part of a God-permitted situation which will ultimately result in my good.

Forgiveness says, "As Christ forgave, I also forgive." His own crucifixion was seen by our Lord in this way. He realized that those who hurt did not understand why they hurt him. He also viewed their act as God-permitted. Those standing around didn't understand the brutality, but Jesus knew that this act would work for good, the salvation of the world.

By an act of your will, begin now to forgive. Forgive even though you don't feel like it.

Continued Effort

The third step requires a continued effort.

Once, I cleared my conscience with regard to a person I resented. A few weeks later someone mentioned that person's name, and there arose within me some resentful feelings. I was shocked and angered! I thought the issue was resolved. It seemed that every positive effort I made to forgive had been for nothing. I said to God, "But, I forgive, I forgive!" In moments the feelings disappeared. A few days later the feelings appeared again, and in my desperation to deny their presence I prayed again, "But, Lord, I forgive!" It dawned on me that every time the feelings came and I attacked them with a renewed commitment to forgive, the resentful feelings vanished. Reflection on what happened revealed the following: 1) Consciously, I forgave; 2) subconsciously, I had old feelings of resentment; and 3) continued conscious forgiving eventually washed out the subconscious resentment fixations that aroused my emotions. Subsequently I realized that my subconscious was being dealt with by the cleansing of the Word (Eph. 4:32). See diagram, next page.

My emotions, like warning lights, kept indicating that I still had resentment on a subconscious level and needed cleansing. In a few weeks every feeling of resentment was gone. Today there is love in my heart for that person.

Let me suggest some actions you can take to neutralize feelings of resentment triggered on a subconscious level: 1) Pray for that person (Matt. 5:44); 2) do something good for that person; 3) say something good to or about that person (Luke 6:27).

Develop a strategy of resolving resentment. Clear your conscience by listing your offenses and asking forgiveness. Consciously forgive that person by visualizing him in your mind and saying, "I forgive you." Listen to what you say! It's good for you. Finally, make a list of all the things you intend and will do to exercise a conscious attitude of forgiveness.

Forgiveness: A conscious deliberate act of the will releasing a person of any and all debts.

Subconscious mental fixations (old man) of resentment often reside after willfully forgiving someone. Later the fixation often 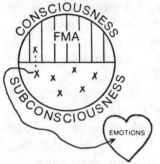 surfaces when probed by association or an incident involving the person you forgave. This triggers the feeling of resentment. Willful, conscious, reaffirmation of your F.M.A. (Forgiving Mental Attitude) toward the offender on the authority of God's Word cleanses the mental fixation. (Eph. 4:32; Luke 23:24; John 15:3).

6
Grappling with Guilt

He looked emaciated. Only months before he had been a picture of health. The man's considerable weight loss deeply concerned his pastor, and insightfully the pastor asked the weak and emaciated visitor if he were experiencing guilt. Verbally probing around, the pastor struck a nerve called adultery. "Oh," the man cried, "that's my problem, that's my problem!"

King David of the Bible was a great leader. He had an appealing personality and devoted his life to doing God's will, but in a time of weakness, in the zenith of his reign, David sinned two dreadful sins: adultery and murder. He cleverly covered his sinful deeds, but what he secretly hid God shouted to the housetops.

One thing that was overwhelming to David through all of this was his guilt. In Psalm 38:1-13 (RSV), he described the pangs of conviction, ("arrows"); depression, ("burden too heavy"); physical deterioration, ("no soundness"); anxiety, ("bowed down"); and weak feelings, ("utterly spent") that are associated with guilt. He said he no longer had a cheerful countenance, ("light of my eyes"); and he found himself loathsome, ("foul and fester"); and offensive to others. As a "deaf man" he no longer heard from God; the guilt was unbearable. In Psalm 51:3, he agonized that his sin was ever present, would never leave him.

Guilt Is the Result of a Torn Conscience

When the God-given conscience is raging in the Christian's life he should be grateful. The psychic pain inflicted by the Holy Spirit telling us something is sin is a gift of God. A person born of the Spirit (John 3) has a quickened conscience, and a new Christian often feels guilt more easily than before he was born again. He should be more sensitive, since the conscience in his spirit is now given new life.

Pseudo-Guilt

Some people think they've sinned because they feel guilty, when their guilt is actually unwarranted. This guilt springs from a trained or man-made conscience. For instance, one may feel guilty about eating ham because he was taught it was wrong. Dr. Paul Tournier, author of *Guilt or Grace*, said his wife sheepishly remarked while dining one night that she felt a little guilty about cutting into the butter on the wrong end because a well-mannered person would have taken the butter from the end already begun! Life may very well be seasoned with guilt because of what we've been taught in the area of mores, not Bible-based morals. Much guilt can be resolved by claiming freedom from the "law" and committing ourselves to Bible principles.

Dealing with Guilt

It seems that some people attempt to overcome guilt by *accelerating life*. The faster things go the less guilt is felt. Perhaps this is why they live fast lives, take amphetamines ("speed"), or "work themselves to death."

Others try to overcome guilt by *slowing everything down.* These people sleep a lot, take depressants, and drink alcohol. If everything is slowed down *enough* they avoid the cruel feelings of guilt.

Another class of people resolves guilt by *blaming others* for their actions. They insist their spouses drove them to wrongdoing or blame their parents for wretched childhoods that resulted in lives of sin they simply couldn't help.

One more group of guilty persons *attempts to get everyone to do what they're doing* to relieve their guilt. Often a guilt-ridden alcoholic will try to get his wife to drink with him. Her abstinence only makes him feel more guilty.

God's Method

Proper confession on the basis of 1 John 1:9, "If we confess our sins, he is faithful and just to forgive us our sins, and to cleanse us from all unrighteousness," is the first step in resolving guilt.

Confession is not confession if at the same time you try to *justify your actions.* "I couldn't help it," or "they talked me into it," cannot accompany confession. *You* decided to sin, not someone else. You must accept the full responsibility of your action.

A troubled lady was seeking relief from guilt. When I asked her why she felt guilty she said she wasn't sure. Perhaps she wasn't a very good mother. "In what ways are you not a good mother?" I inquired. Her answers were vague. "How long have you felt this way?" She thought her tormenting feelings went back at least six years. "Did you do something at that time which caused deep regret?" "Yes," she said, "but I asked the Lord to forgive me. You see, what I did was something I did when I wasn't feeling well. My friends talked me into it." Instantly, I knew what her problem was. She may have confessed, but she din't confess properly. She was not accepting the full responsibility for her action because she was blaming both her sickness and her friends for what she did. "Tell me," I asked, "did your friends make the decision to sin or did you? Even though they influenced you, who actually did the sinning?" She replied, "I did."

"In 1 John 1:9," I went on to explain, "the word 'confess' literally means 'to agree' or 'say back.' Otherwise, the Holy Spirit says you sinned and you should fully agree. You told the Holy Spirit you participated, but you really didn't agree with him that you were totally responsible for your sin. You pushed that over on someone else. He wants you to agree with him that you sinned the whole sin and were totally responsible for the terrible deed."

She said, "Could I pray now?" With her head on my desk, she poured out her bitter confession, assuming full responsibility for what she did. Looking up, she smiled and walked out a changed woman. She had six years of unwarranted suffering all because she refused to accept full responsibility for her sin.

Confession is not confession if you *rationalize your actions.* Be honest about how bad the sin is. Don't for a moment think that the sin is little. James said to offend in one little point is to break the whole law. David's sin was enormous. Any sin is enormous, because any sin damages our fellowship with God.

I recall a woman who finally got release from her guilt when she confessed her sin of abortion. She no longer rationalized it as the right thing to do. In her mind, it had been more convenient for her and everyone else to take the life of that fetus. But all the rationalization in the world could not remove her guilt. Her head said it was right, but her heart knew better and would not rest until she would admit her abortion was wrong. I nearly gasped when she prayed, "Oh God, forgive me for taking the life of that child. I murdered, and I ask you to forgive me."

She confessed it exactly like it was. It was then that she ceased to be tormented by guilt. She was set free.

It's important that I agree with God about my sin and realize I'm totally responsible for it. Then I humbly receive his forgiveness and cleansing, not because he must honor me but because he must honor his Word.

I Can't Forgive Myself

There's a great difference between "heart condemnation" (1 John 3:19-22) and "God condemnation" (Rom. 8:1). If we are born again, God convicts us but doesn't condemn us. The word in 1 John 3:21 translated "condemn" actually means to "know something against." The heart will remind you of wrong by expressing itself in guilt. Guilt is the indicator, the red flag, that says I've damaged my relationship with God. "If our heart condemns us not, then have we confidence toward God," (v. 21). To have no confidence toward God means we can't look him in the eye. Heart condemnation is one of the greatest hindrances to prayer (1 John 3:22).

When I can't forgive myself I'm actually saying, "God, you may forgive, but I can't. I'm a better judge of this sin than you." Not to forgive is to put oneself above God. It is an interesting form of pride to say I refuse to do something God is more than willing to do.

Often we feel unworthy of forgiveness and decide we need to suffer a few more days, weeks, or months. This is to say, "God, your payment on the cross was insufficient; I'll have to pay the balance. Your suffering was not quite thorough enough."

God Won't Forgive?

Occasionally someone will insist that God can't forgive him for the terrible thing he did. This is another strange form of pride. It's the kind of pride that says his sin is larger than God's grace. How could any sin be larger than the infinite grace of our Lord? Just as God has more answers than we have problems, he has more grace than we have sins.

Overcoming Guilt Recurrence

What is the key to overcoming recurring guilt? It is obvious that guilt is one of the most powerful negative emotions that rages in man's heart. It drains and weakens. It saps spiritual, psychological, and physical strength. With this in mind, it is then easy to understand why Satan tries to inflict guilt if he can. Revelation 12:10 says that Satan is an accuser of the brethren and accuses night and day, with the expectation that the Christian will become preoccupied, diverted, and weakened. How does one brace himself against Satan's attacks? Satan is cunning in rattling old skeletons from the past.

Confess It

Make sure you confess your sin properly. Agree with God about your sin. Assume the full responsibility of your disgusting act. But receive God's forgiveness immediately and enjoy full release (1 John 1:9).

Don't Dwell On It

To forget is extremely important. Of course, one cannot erase the memory. Martin Luther was reported to have said, "The birds can fly over your head but they need not make a nest in your hair." Every time Satan dangles that old forgiven sin in your face, don't allow yourself to dwell on it. The Bible declares that God will remember our sins no more. He forgets, and we should,

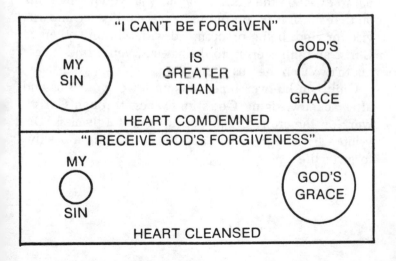

too. In Philippians 3:13, we read, "Forgetting those things which are behind." That's Scripture, and that's God's will. To dwell on the forgiven past is opposed to God's will and, therefore, sin. When we begin to dwell on old, forgiven sins, we have a new sin to confess. So, confess that, too, and press on.

Press On

In Philippians 3:14, it says we should "press on" (RSV). The key to forgetting is moving. If I insist that you not think about a gray elephant, invariably in your effort not to think about it you find yourself obsessed with the thought. If I should describe fresh-baked, homemade short-cake heaped with luscious, homegrown strawberries and whipped cream, somehow that positive image is so appealing and appetizing that you don't think about a gray elephant. If all you do is spend time trying not to dwell on the sin that haunts you, you'll only think on that sin. But if you put in its place diligence and service for God, being preoccupied with winning others to Christ and ministering to their needs, you'll find it easy not to dwell on the sins of the past.

Guilt can be overcome. Make a list of your sins and after acknowledging God's forgiveness through Christ's work on the cross, *thank* God for that forgiveness. Develop a list of "press-ons" and begin building a positive forgiven life.

7
Attacking Anxiety

The envelope was from the Internal Revenue Service. The letter simply stated that the foundation of which I'm executive director was to be examined. The examination required my presence, the foundation's books, canceled checks, and other documents. This organization has been an instrument through which God has blessed families, and somehow the more I thought about this examination the more it bothered me. What had we done wrong? The more I pursued this line of thinking, the more my stomach began to churn. I really felt torn up inside.

Suddenly I thought, "If we did nothing wrong, why should I be upset?" Well, that made me feel better until Satan said, "But, suppose you neglected to do something that was important? That could get you into a lot of trouble. You could lose your influence and perhaps your ministry."

Finally, I went to the Lord, he reminded me of the principles I share with others who are faced with anxiety. God gave me a special release, and I found myself unusually relaxed during the three weeks of waiting. The meeting took place, and the foundation was given a clean bill of health. Later the man from the I.R.S. took me out and bought me a cup of coffee. The meeting ended better than expected.

The Bible words related to worry or anxiety appear in the King James Version in such forms as care and careful, "be careful for nothing," and are all derived from the Greek word *merimna*. The literal meaning of its verb form is "to divide," "to pull in different directions," and "to tear or rip apart." These meanings are a fairly concise description of how anxiety actually feels.

Anxiety takes its toll physically, sometimes causing visceral pain, ulcers, headaches, and dysentery. I've seen people break out in hives as they share their anxieties.

Feelings of anxiety are good, because they are symptoms of correctable problems or a life-style needing some scriptural adjustments. If an individual does not see his anxiety as a flashing signal telling him to correct a life pattern, the anxiety becomes his master. Some try certain alternative cures. Giving partial symptomatic relief, antidepressants and tranquilizers become a way of life. Alcohol is a popular alternative. But these actually only intensify anxiety. If a person already has financial problems and spends more of his money on pills and alcohol, his anxiety is only complicated.

It's important to realize that giving in to anxiety is wrong; indeed, it is a direct violation of God's plan for our lives. God did not intend for us to be anxiety-ridden. Did not Jesus directly, clearly say, "Do not be anxious" (Matt. 6:25, RSV)? But isn't a little anxiety good? Doesn't a little anxiety keep a person on his toes, cautious, and responsible? Apparently, the Lord didn't think so. Paul, inspired as he wrote to the Philippians, said, "Be careful [anxious] for nothing" (4:6). That's quite clear. Anxiety and worry are sin.

Once my wife and I were riding along when she

looked over at me and said, "What are you worried about, Ralph?" I said I wasn't worried, only concerned about a church problem that needed to be handled properly. As you can see, I rationalized away worry and regarded my actions as right. But, insightfully, my wife said, "Well, whatever you call it, it's not good for you." I had no answer but clearly knew my reactions to the church problems were wrong. Confession was in order. There was a better way of tackling the problems. They could be worked out with joy, not anxiety.

Anxiety is the evidence of several things. It is an evidence that I may not have done everything I should have about my problem. There is no substitute for obedience. It also suggests that I may not have looked to God for answers, or I may not have trusted God to work out the situation if it's completely out of my control.

Anxiety could be the result of procrastination. I certainly feel torn when it occurs to me I have something to do and my time has run out. I've always loved life and enjoyed being around people. While others toiled over their books in school, I socialized. The night before my tests I'd cram until dawn. Term papers and manuscripts were begun the day before they were due. You can imagine how I felt. However, I got tired of the anxiety that went with procrastination and decided to get things done before time. There's a unique joy that accompanies the relaxed moments between the time you complete something and the time it's due.

Jesus said "do not be anxious about tomorrow" (Matt. 6:34, RSV). In other words, don't spend your energies distressing yourself over something in the future; pour your energies into top priority projects today. When you procrastinate, there is always that gnawing sensation that says you ought to be doing what needs to be done. As the time draws closer, the gnawing sensation reaches panic proportions, and the once bearable anxiety now looms so great that it is difficult to be imaginative, insightful, or thorough. The job completed is never your best work. This produces another anxiety because you did inferior work when you know you could have done a better job.

Abraham faced life's assignments admirably when God asked him to offer up Isaac. "And Abraham rose up early in the morning . . . and took . . . Isaac his son" (Gen. 22:3). One secret to avoiding anxiety is to get things done right away, early. Do the important things first.

Anxiety is also an evidence of badly-arranged priorities. Sometimes we rush into doing the urgent and put aside the important. Jesus gave a solid answer for anxiety in the Sermon on the Mount when he said, "Seek ye first the kingdom of God, and his righteousness; and all these things shall be added unto you" (Matt. 6:33). We'll put off prayer and wade into a day as though it all depended on us and as though God didn't exist. I've also seen people frustrated in trying to find scriptural answers finally go back to the world's way of doing of things, only to complicate their anxieties.

I have a friend who worked as a management consultant for a major oil company. He authored manuals on functional management and personnel development. One of the finest gifts he gave me was the advice to "write down six priorities for the day, arrange them from the most important to the least important, and work off the top of the list." You can't imagine how this has allevi- ated anxiety in my life.

I once heard that it takes 90 percent of your working time to do 10 percent of your work (most difficult responsibilities) and 10 percent of your time to do 90 percent of your work (easiest responsibilities). Most people do the easiest things (90 percent) first but take 100 percent of their time doing them. However, when the difficult things are done first, the easiest things seem to get done almost on their own.

Somebody once told me I should have three baskets. In the top basket I should put things that must be done now. In the second basket I should put the things that must be done later, and in the third basket I should put everything else. When the first basket is emptied, he advised, go to the next. In time, the things in the third basket don't seem important or get done without con- scious effort. You'll feel much better if you get to impor- tant things first. Naturally, time must be taken to decide what's important, and that's where proper plan- ning comes in.

Anxiety is sometimes an evidence of poor planning. Soloman said, "If the iron be blunt, and he not whet [sharpen] the edge, then must he put to more strength" (Eccl. 10:10).

I find it relaxing if I take time to plan. Why make sev- eral trips when with good planning you can make one?

Sometimes we have to delegate work as the result of planning. A mother who takes a few minutes to write chore lists for her children gives them something produc- tive to do but also relieves herself of some work she doesn't have time to accomplish. When you delegate you enrich someone's life by giving him an opportunity to be productive.

In James 4:13-15, the writer wrote that we shouldn't announce a decision to do anything or go anywhere without saying, "If the Lord wills." On the surface this seems to say that one shouldn't plan. But, to the contrary, it says *we need to plan according to God's will.* Planning requires finding the mind of God, a Word from the Lord. A person who plans according to God's will can overcome anxiety if he really puts his trust in what God says.

Anxiety may be an evidence of prayerlessness. How the Lord wants us to commune with him! One man said, "In the morning my first thoughts are of God as I kneel in prayer, and by my bed at night I pray with my last thought on him again before I sleep."

Someone said, "But why pray when you can worry?" Anxiety displaces considerable prayer time. It's like robbing God of something special that should be dedicated to him.

Through prayer we can release our worries to him. A preacher lay awake through the night tossing and turning, anxiously pondering something. In the night he heard the Lord say, "Son, Why don't you go to sleep and let me worry about this one?" So, he did.

Paul's formula for overcoming worry is "Be careful [anxious] for nothing," don't worry about anything, "but in every thing by prayer," a factual request, "and supplication . . . ," a request including facts and feelings, "let your requests be made known unto God," (Phil. 4:6). The word *prayer* is an objective term, whereas *supplication* is a subjective term. So, when you pray tell God what you're thinking and release to God exactly how you feel. This is a great way to release both mind and emotions so God can give peace. Additionally, in this new state of mind, a person is in better condition to receive answers and insights.

Anxiety is also a result of *little praise.* When Paul said, "Be careful for nothing; but in every thing by prayer and supplication . . . let your requests be made known to God," he also included "with thanksgiving." A fretful, anxious mind is an ungrateful mind. Here is an opportunity to give thanks in all things. (Also see 1 Thess. 15:18.)

My family and I were making a trip when our car broke down. The mechanic said it would cost $100 to repair it. We didn't have the money, and so we were stuck 500 miles from home. We found a motel and settled down with a good case of anxiety. Now we had traveled all over the country sharing with people the great principle of giving thanks in all things, but somehow we forgot that truth. The next morning I found myself pacing the floor working myself into a king-sized headache. Then it came to me, "thanks in all things." Together my wife and I knelt in gratitude to God thanking him for the opportunity to see himself proven adequate in our lives. We calmly went to the garage and waited for the car to be fixed. Our children were small and behaved exceptionally well. Before the day was over God supplied a miraculous way for us to pay the bill and go home. He even took into consideration that the bill would be $225 and not $100.

The end result of praying with thanksgiving is "and the peace of God, which passeth all understanding shall keep your hearts and minds through Christ Jesus" (Phil. 4:7).

Finally, we must recognize anxiety as our way of saying, "God doesn't care," or "God, you can't control the issues of my life," or "God, you don't have the answers." Anxiety is often the evidence that we don't trust God.

In review, let us look at the positive steps we can take to resolve our anxiety.

First, confess the sin of anxiety and ask him to cleanse you of this attitude.

Next, take time to list the things that are vexing you and determine whether they are the result of procrastination, badly-arranged priorities, or poor planning.

If none of the above relate to your anxiety or if they do relate, take time to pray and praise. In your anxious moment try "casting all your care upon him; for he careth for you" (1 Pet. 5:7).

If procrastination, badly-arranged priorities, or poor planning relate to your situation, begin to correct them now. Above all, spend time in giving thanks in this time of anxiety. Isolate that which vexes you and offer it up as a praise offering. Then stand back and let God be God.

I visited a young man in the hospital where they were preparing to remove two-thirds of his ulcer-eaten stomach. He was the bodyguard for a mayor in a large Eastern city. He told me about all the things that were weighing on him. It seemed that he had more than his share, including a wife dying with cancer, a little girl who was molested, and the pressures of work.

I said, "Don, if I could locate a man in this city who would solve every problem you have, what would you be willing to do?" "I would cut off my right arm for such a man," he replied. "Well," I said, "I want to introduce him to you right now. His name is Jesus." In the next moments I saw a grown man quietly weep as he gave his life to Christ. His wife came into the room. They hugged each other as our Lord himself held them in a loving embrace. Don had found a new relationship with the Savior and problem-solver. What I saw was indeed a miracle. His surgery went as planned. A few days later in his home he showed how God was solving each problem. The Lord even gave his wife extra time to take care of the family.

It certainly pays to turn it all over to the Lord. Let him heal your anxious soul and help you work out the anxiety-provoking situations of your life.

8
An Answer for Anger

An elderly lady sat in her car by the side of the road. She was visibly shaken. When the police arrived, the story was told. She had apparently eased into traffic when a pick-up truck nearly hit her from behind. The driver of the truck was furious. Shouting obscenities, he drove alongside, ramming her car in the side. When the lady finally came to a stop the pick-up sped on, the driver still cursing her.

Anger is a powerful emotion. Vented, it can destroy. Harbored, it takes its toll internally.

"The famous physiologist, John Hunter, knew what anger could do to his heart. 'The first scoundrel that gets me angry will kill me!' Sometime later at a medical meeting, a speaker made assertions that incensed Hunter. As he stood up and bitterly attacked the speaker, his anger caused such a contraction of the blood vessels in his heart that he fell dead."[1]

In his book *None of These Diseases* S. I. McMillen, M.D., says that anger stimulates the adrenal glands, and an excessive amount of adrenaline over an extended period of time has a deteriorating effect on the body. The lion has a life-span of about twenty-five years. In contrast, the crocodile can live many years after the lion's bones are dried and bleached. The difference? The lion has exceptionally large adrenal glands. The crocodile's are very small. The pacing lion responds quickly to stress and alarm. The crocodile often lies motionless and undisturbed with life. Dr. George Crile of the Crile Clinic discovered that longevity is directly related to one's ability to cope with stress and irritation.[1]

Two Kinds of Anger

The New Testament in its original language has two words used for anger. *Thumos* tends to be an anger that is expressed. It blows. *Orge* is usually an internalized anger. It broods.

Is Anger Wrong?

From the Bible we realize that all anger is not wrong. Indeed, we read, "Be ye angry, and sin not" (Eph. 4:26). It is possible to be angry and sin. It is also possible to be angry and not sin. To become angered over sin is not wrong. To become angered because one's personal rights have been violated is almost always wrong.

When Is Anger Wrong?

Numerous Scriptures teach that anger *expressed too soon* is sin. "Be . . . slow to wrath" (Jas. 1:19,20). Other verses to study are Proverbs 14:29; 16:32; 19:11. Wrong anger equals *anger plus impatience.* Too many times people "blow up" before thinking. They vent anger and lose control. Someone has defined *temperamental* as 95 percent temper and 5 percent mental.

I heard a loud knock on my door. I opened it and there stood Joe. He said, "Preacher, I need help." What he had to say was laced with some rather crude language. He told me he was having trouble with his anger at work and home. He had broken some furniture and, to top it off, had smashed his favorite moustache coffee mug. Well, that did it. Joe's problems with anger out of control went back a long way. Fortunately, Joe trusted Christ as his Savior and then began to apply scriptural principles to his problem of anger. Later I saw his wife, who wanted to divorce him. When I asked her how Joe was doing she said with mild disgust, "Oh, he reads his Bible every day." She was fast losing her reasons to divorce him.

Anger is also wrong when *expressed too late.* Often when issues are dead, a brooding, resentful person finally expresses his anger. "Let not the sun go down upon your wrath" (Eph. 4:26).

I've talked to couples with a communication breakdown. Often it's a surprise when a mate discovers that the other's coldness, nagging, picking, and abstinence go back to an incident of years ago. One mate forgot it, but the other didn't. Fostering anger certainly does damage.

An impotent husband finally shared his lack of response toward his wife in a counseling session. He often worked twelve to sixteen hours a day and would come home to find his wife talking on the phone, the dishes piled high in the sink, and the house a total disaster. This angered him. Being a mild-mannered type, he would suggest helping her clean up, but all the time he was fuming. Later in the evening when she acted affectionate toward him, he found her repulsive and disgusting. I asked him why he didn't talk to her about his feelings when he was angered by the appearance of the house. "You're kidding!" he said. "Do you want me to talk to her about it?" I asked. "Be my guest," he replied. So, I did, the next session. Whew! Talk about a reaction! I could appreciate why he didn't want to approach her. Her anger was externalized and unpredictable. His anger was internalized and usually expressed too late. It surfaced in his impotence. Brooding in anger, he was stubborn and selfish.

A man on the West Coast bought a beautiful car, but it had a squeak. The dealer didn't fix it, and it really bothered him. The squeak was coming from the back, and so he asked his wife to drive the car while he got in the trunk. She apparently got their signals confused. When he tapped on the trunk to stop, she thought he meant to go faster. Back in the trunk he became violently sick. When she didn't hear him tap anymore, she drove back to the house, opened the trunk, and walked into the house. He rolled out and fell into the grass as sick as a dog. He was so angry, he stayed outside until he was sure that his wife had gone to bed. Then he went inside, cleaned up, and retired. He never said a word of any of this to his wife. Twelve years later the husband shared his story of resentment to a minister friend. His wife was shocked. She had no idea why her husband had been so distant all those years.

Brooding anger is often linked to resentment. Already we've looked at the serious consequences related to the existence of this emotion.

In Matthew 5:22, we discover a third form of wrong anger. Jesus said we shouldn't be angry without a cause. Wrong anger is *anger minus* a reason.

So much anger is expressed without a just cause. People get angry for the most insignificant reasons. I remember the wife whose husband was going to school. She scraped together a handful of change and went to the laundromat. It was the last money before payday. As she sat waiting for the clothes to dry her husband appeared and asked her for the leftover change so he could buy a Pepsi. There wasn't enough. He went into orbit. "Don't you know I always have a Pepsi before going to class?" Anger minus a reason.

Ephesians 4:26-29 indicates that anger is often expressed in speech, and therefore anger that is verbalized to intimidate and tear down is wrong. Wrong anger is *anger minus grace.*

"Let no corrupt communication proceed out of your mouth, but that which is good to the use of edifying, that it may minister grace to the hearers" (v. 29).

Since my son is in Little League baseball, I attend as many games as possible. If you want to see anger, go to a Little League baseball game. I've seen coaches come off their benches red-faced, fists shaking, and jaws flapping at incredible speeds. How they can say so much and make any sense is beyond me. Normally, they don't. The umpire is embarrassed. The kid called out is flustered, and parents look on with disbelief. The umpire hangs in there, and the coach kicks dirt all the way back to the bench, turning every few steps, uttering phrases you can't quite make out. Who is helped by all this? No one. On the other hand, an angry coach could quietly walk up to the umpire and calmly respond to the decision. Objectively, two men could work it out. The umpire could look at his rule book and see he's right. The coach could walk back, having expressed his anger the right way. That's anger plus grace.

How to Avoid Wrong Anger

Proverbs 22:24 teaches us that we should not make friendships with angry people, lest we learn their ways and encounter a snare to our souls. We should *avoid* as much as possible *associating with angry people.*

My son and I looked at this verse when he was trying to resolve a relationship with a little fellow who got angry when he didn't get his own way. A vein would stand out on his forehead and he'd rant and rave until all the other kids gave in to what he wanted. I told my son that it would be best not to associate with him, or he would find himself doing the same things. We prayed about it and especially for the angry playmate. Fortunately, the little guy improved and became a close companion to my son.

Second, we can avoid wrong anger by *living a life of obedience.* Cain's anger which led to murder (Gen. 4:3-7) began with disobedience. Disobedient people are like pressure cookers ready to blow.

One thing is extremely important to me. I want to put in productive days at work. If I don't, I find myself edgy and irritable. Disappointed with my behavior, I am tempted to be hard on those around me.

On a large scale, a person with a life-style of sin and disobedience is irritable, too. He's always on the verge of anger, and too often displays it irrationally.

A life of obedience helps a person feel good about himself, helps him to feel calm and relaxed. The hair-triggered individual usually reveals a basic problem of disobedience and a life-style of rebellion.

Third, we discover that a person who is always concerned about his rights is opening himself to a life of anger. *A man overly concerned about his rights is an angry man.*

Working with a certain young man, I realized that his violent outbursts were provoked by his rigid demand for rights. Whenever his rights were abused he would become angry. His right to drive down the road without someone getting in his way could be easily violated if someone stopped quickly in front of him. The result? Anger. If someone stepped in line in front of him his right to be next would be violated. Result? Anger.

So much of our anger is the result of claiming rights. Bill Gothard, in his seminar on *Basic Youth Conflicts* often says "Give your rights to God and he will give them back to you as privileges."

So much wrong anger can be avoided by giving our rights to God in loving surrender. Romans 6:13 says, "yield yourselves." Total yielding includes all I claim and all I possess.

If life has only privileges instead of rights I don't become angry when someone stops abruptly in front of me—I thank God for the privilege of having driven for days without an occurrence like this. Isn't it amazing that an event that takes place in a fraction of a second can destroy a whole day? We should enjoy the whole of life and let the little aggravations go.

What If I Feel Angry?

If you should feel angry, it's very possible that your anger is pointing out an incomplete yielding of your rights to God. *Determine whether God has all your rights.*

Second, *anger should be deferred.* Often, holding

one's anger helps to dissipate it. In Proverbs 29:11, we are taught, "A wise man keepeth it in till afterwards." A teammate in football who blows up is often held down by the other players. The cooling-off period helps him regain his senses. Holding on does help.

When Jesus was angered at the abuse of the "house of prayer" (Luke 20:46), he held his anger. John noticed that his Lord spent some time patiently calculating his next moves, holding back until "he had made a scourge of small cords" (John 2:15). In this case, the Lord's anger did not dissipate by holding it. He released it in a perfect, well-thought-out, deliberate manner. His anger was patient and was released properly.

Anger can be released. It can be released through a project, as our Lord did on two occasions (John 2:14-17; Mark 3:5). On the other hand it can be relieved verbally.

Verbal expressions of anger require some guidelines. In Ephesians 4:29 Paul said, "Let no corrupt communication proceed out of your mouth." The word *corrupt* means "rotten." The opposite of *rotten* is *preserved*. When I'm about to verbalize my righteous anger I should ask "Is what I'm about to say preserving?" When we intimidate someone and embarrass him before others are we being preserving?

Paul continued, "but that which is good to the use of edifying." To edify means to "build up." When I verbalize my righteous anger am I building the person up? Am I constructive?

Finally, Paul said "that it may minister grace unto the hearers." Is what I have to say a gift? It should be something the recipient can receive with gratitude. At the time he may not be grateful, but later he should.

Now, here is something for you to do. Take time to list the rights you claim that result in anger. Yield them to God.

If you express anger wrongly there is divine forgiveness and cleansing. Your shame and guilt can be cleansed by appropriating 1 John 1:9. Press on after you've enjoyed that cleansing and gratefully live a life yielded to God.

Notes

1. S. I. McMillen, *None of These Diseases* (New Jersey: Fleming Revell, 1963), p. 71.
2. *Ibid.*, pp. 81-84.

9
Freedom from Fear

Ruth had been bumped around most of her life. Going from one foster home to another, she had learned to fend for herself. She found acceptance on the street. When I talked with her, a young lady in her twenties, I saw a hard and crusted veneer, but underneath was a heart stricken with terror. During the past few years her exposure to drugs and prostitution had brought her into a world of organized crime. Valuable as an informant, she had worked closely with the law in an effort to break up a powerful drug business. She believed there was a contract on her life, and we provided sanctuary for her until a safe place in another city was found.

As I shared with her it was obvious she was ready to receive Chrst—which she did—but not without a struggle. "How can he come into a heart full of so much hate and fear?" she asked. She explained that she was accustomed to carrying a weapon. "I've learned," she added, "it's best to get them before they get you." But, the Lord penetrated her fear and saved her.

The next day a friend and I visited Ruth and found a changed person. When we asked her how she slept, she explained that in the face of danger she had realized an unusual peace. Indeed, this was a "peace that passeth understanding" and "a peace the world cannot give."

Most psychologists agree that fear is one of the first three emotions an infant feels. The other two are love and anger. Fear could be considered a tormentor, but, on the other hand, fear must be viewed as a friend.

Fear is said to express itself in fight or flight. It also freezes. A person may flee a situation, but he may also freeze in a frightening circumstance. My grandfather's death was caused by his immobility after seeing his clothes on fire. An elderly lady over the fence screamed at him, "Charlie, you're on fire." He just stood there. Someone finally got to him, but it was too late. A couple of days later he died in the hospital.

Fear puts fight into people, too. A fearful person may actually appear angry. "Even according to thy fear, so is thy wrath" (Ps. 90:11). Whenever I'm in contact with angry people I try to determine what might be frightening them. A person pushed into responsibilities greater than he can handle confidently will often appear angry, when fear is actually the cause. Like cornered animals, people can be violent when fear overwhelms them.

It is obvious that fear helps us to survive. One of the first words our year-old daughter learned was "hot." As a parent, I was comforted by her obvious fear of the cascading mountain stream near the cabin where I'm now writing. Fear is healthy, but occasionally comes in unreasonable proportions—causing torment and paralysis. One gentleman with an important message to impart was invited across the country to speak, but he wouldn't accept. He was afraid of flying, which cost him countless opportunities of service for the Lord. Some are afraid of making mistakes in front of others and automatically keep themselves from productive ministries. A woman let her mind work overtime as she added up certain coincidences, and she began to think she was being followed as she drove her car. At home she was sure she was being watched. This obsession kept her in terror. Her days and nights were not spent in productive living as a mother and wife, but in futility, defeat, and failure.

The Bible talks about a healthy fear in our relationships to God. Of course, this fear, which is the beginning of knowledge and wisdom, involves an awe and respect for God's authority and ability. A healthy respect for Jehovah God has its benefits. Fear of God has a healing effect (Prov. 3:7-8). God reveals his secrets and shares valuable insights with those who fear him (Ps. 25:14) and guarantees his watchful care (Ps. 33:18). Often the fear of God produced by the Holy Spirit's convicting power has brought a rebellious person into sweet fellowship with God. The fear of not having him, the fear of eternal separation without him, the fear of not going to heaven (John 16:8) are healthy fears which often bring hard, stubborn, wayward souls into God's loving embrace.

I have known of individuals who think every adversity is a punitive action by the Lord. They live in constant fear. This is unnecessary. For the Christian, adversity is not a vindictive act by God toward his child. "There is therefore now no condemnation to them which are in Christ Jesus" (Rom. 8:1). God does discipline. His discipline, however, is a correction process, not a punitive process. He disciplines in love. The discipline is not exactly joyous; indeed, it is grievous, but its end result is the "peaceable fruit of righteousness" (Heb. 12:11). God's objective is to win our will. As we become compliant and yielded, the discipline ceases. He never punishes us for what he's forgiven. Indeed he remembers our sins no more. However, after discipline we do gain a healthy fear that keeps us walking in his ways.

My children laugh with me, and we play together. I'm met at the door with hugs and kisses. Often our times together abound with unconfined joy. They know I love them deeply and would give my life for them. But sessions of discipline in which I've soundly spanked them have put in them a special fear for their father, a healthy fear. A special look and tone of voice snaps them instantly into an attitude of obedience, from the oldest to the youngest. I'm not angry, but I'm serious. They never have to test my love after that kind of look. God's discipline is administered more perfectly, so if "we have had fathers of our flesh which corrected us, and we gave them reverence: shall we not much rather be in subjection unto the Father?" (Heb. 12:9).

Consequences of Fear

Here are a few consequences of fear.

In the first place, unhealthy fear is a dynamic much like faith. Indeed it often expresses itself as the opposite of faith. Job said, "The thing which I greatly feared is come upon me, and that which I was afraid of is come unto me" (Job 3:25). This principle should cause us to have a healthy respect for fear. The very things we often express in fear come upon us. How many times have we said after a reversal, "I was afraid it would come to this" or "I was afraid this would happen." Job may have said to his wife one day, "I'm afraid that someone is going to steal our cattle," or he may have said to a neighbor, "I've a fine family, but I'm always afraid something is going to happen to those kids of mine." Looking at the clouds one day he may have said to one of his servants, "I'm afraid of these seasonal storms. One of those winds could easily destroy my house." Every one of those things happened to him. Satan honored that fear. God honors faith, but also has an answer for the fear that brings torment and trouble into our lives.

A lady lamenting her recent divorce said to me, "I was afraid of divorce the day we got married." Her mind was trained toward that goal, and she finally reached it by fear. It's amazing how many things we do to help us achieve our fears when our minds are occupied with the things we dread. Again, Solomon said, "As [a man] thinketh in his heart, so is he" (Prov. 23:7). The man with dreams who steadfastly thinks on his dreams somehow accomplishes those dreams. The man who dreads and refuses to clear those fears from his mind somehow sees accomplished what he dreaded.

A second consequence of fear is the debilitating effect it has on our lives. Fear has to be one of the reasons for laziness and irresponsibility. "The slothful man saith, there is a lion in the way; a lion is in the streets" (Prov. 26:13). Fear makes a man lazy. "He that observeth the wind shall not sow; and he that regardeth the clouds shall not reap" (Eccl. 11:4).

The person who is afriad of traffic and refuses to drive in it will have a difficult time being productive in life.

Every time we take a step we might fall, but that doesn't mean we should be so cautious as to sit all day. More people are hurt by fear than we can imagine. Fear could have kept Moses from delivering Israel from slavery. Fear could have kept Gideon from being a champion for the people. Fear could have kept Jeremiah from warning a country bent on destruction. Fear has and will make parents irresponsible, children forever dependent, businessmen paupers, preachers failures, and leaders weak. Think what could happen to struggling local churches, to failing families, and defeated servants of God if all fear could be removed.

Cause of Fear

What's the cause of fear? There is one element always present in fear, and that's self-centeredness. No matter how you look at it fear is rooted in a selfish attitude. "I don't want to look bad." "I don't want to get hurt." "I don't want to appear foolish." "I don't want to fail." "I might faint." "I can't stand it." "I can't speak." "I might get hit." "I," "I," I," "I," "I." Acts of true bravery have been those done with total disregard for self and total concern for the well-being of others. The elder John said, "There is no fear in love" (1 John 4:18), because love is unselfish.

Unhealthy fear, I believe, is an attitude from Satan. Paul said to Timothy, "God hath not given us the spirit of fear; but of power, and of love, and of a sound mind" (2 Tim. 1:7). If cowardice is not from God, where, then, does it come from? As it is Satan's desire to have us experience unwarranted feeling of guilt (Rev. 12:10), he also

wants us to be overwhelmed by other dark emotions such
as resentment (2 Cor. 2:10-11), and definitely fear. The
spirit of fear keeps us incapacitated in doing God's will.
Timothy's fear was in sharing a clear bold witness for
Christ. He was experiencing timidity in telling others the
"good news" of Christ's redemptive work on the cross
and his ability to make new creatures out of old sinners.
This kind of fear and other fears resulting in our defeat,
irresponsibility, and lack of productivity are from Satan.

Another cause of fear is disobedience. Fear often
springs out of a life of rebellion, dishonesty, fraud, and
disobedience in general. Adam and Eve registered the
first known fear (Gen. 3:6-11) when they sinned in the
garden. David's paranoia was related to two sins in his
transgressions toward Uriah (Ps. 38:12). A member of
the British Parliament played a practical joke on some of
his colleagues. On a note which he gave to each of his
friends, he simply wrote "It's out!" with no signature.
Within twenty-four hours each of these men fled to other
countries. "The wicked flee when no man pursueth; but
the righteous are bold as a lion" (Prov. 28:1).

A man spent considerable time in a mental institution
because of his paranoia. He thought everyone was after
him, including the Communists and the FBI. He
couldn't trust a soul. When he came to see me after his
last stay in the mental ward, I thought it might be good
for him to list the sins that haunted him continually. At
our next session together he produced a list several pages
long naming wicked, vile, disgusting, repulsive acts. No
wonder he was afraid! With that kind of record I'd think
everyone was after me, too. The one complete answer for

his fears was forgiveness. David, the psalmist, knew. "Blessed is he whose transgression is forgiven, whose sin is covered" (Ps. 32:1).

A Cure for Fear

What is the cure for fear? Let's first look at 2 Timothy 1:7. "God hath not given to us the spirit of fear; but [an antidote] of power, and of love and of a sound mind."

Whenever a person fears, he's usually overcome by a sense of helplessness. He needs power and the knowledge that he has the wherewithal to face a situation. We say we "can't" or we walk into a frightening ordeal already consenting to failure. Now, God abounds where we lack. "[His] grace is sufficient" said the apostle Paul in 2 Corinthians 12:9. This knowledge gave him the boldness to say, "I can do all things through Christ which strengtheneth me" (Phil. 4:13). He could confidently say that if God wanted him to do anything he could, with the strength Christ would provide. The writer of the book of Hebrews wrote, "For he hath said, I will never leave thee, nor forsake thee. So that we may boldly say, The Lord is my helper, and I will not fear what man shall do unto me" (Heb. 13:5-6).

The Bible is full of promises that should assure us of power, of strength, of might in the face of situations that are beyond human capacities to tackle. Read them and be strong.

"Fear thou not; for I am with thee: be not dismayed; for I am thy God: I will strengthen thee; yea, I will help thee; yea, I will uphold thee with the right hand of my righteousness," (Isa. 4:10).

"God is our refuge and strength, a very present help in trouble. Therefore will not we fear" (Ps. 46:1-2).

"But the Lord said unto me, Say not I am a child: for thou shalt go to all that I shall send thee, and whatsoever I command thee thou shalt speak. Be not afraid of their faces; for I am with thee to deliver thee, saith the Lord" (Jer. 1:7-8).

"And, lo, I am with you alway, even unto the end of the world. Amen" (Matt. 28:20).

The first step in overcoming fear is to recognize and use the power God supplies.

Second, God has given us *love* as an antidote to fear. The disciple John said, "Love casteth out fear" (1 John 4:18). People are useless to their families, to their friends, and others needing their help because they don't love. Fear outweighs any love they have or they would shake loose and get involved.

An old legend goes like this: An eagle swooped down into a village and carried away an infant to the rocky crag above where the eagle's nest was perched. The villagers ran to the cliff and someone cried, "Who will go after the baby?" Grown men looked away and young boys stared at the ground. A woman passed through the stunned crowd and began to scale the treacherous rocks. Fighting off the eagle, she secured the child in her arms and made her descent to an applauding crowd. What gave that woman such courage? What motivation sent her on such a dangerous mission, in total disregard for her own life and safety? It was love. She was the child's mother!

For a time my wife and I ministered to some underprivileged people in a dangerous part of town. At times I walked those streets at night and wondered why I had no fear, until a college student, out of curiosity, asked to go there with me. When we arrived, I noticed he was scared to death. Some young men saw his fear and began to gang up on him. Stepping between them, I got him out of there and took him home. The difference? He didn't love those people. They were just objects of curiosity. When you love, fear leaves.

In another chapter is a treatment on love and how to experience it. This scriptural approach to love will cast out the torment of fear.

If you love, you'll do things for others regardless of the dangers you think are lurking in your way.

Another antidote to fear is a *sound mind* or *self-control.* A sound mind is an informed mind.

Often times people overcome fears by simply gaining information. Ignorance breeds fear and superstition.

A lady who received Christ wanted to publicly confess her new relationship to the Lord by going forward in a church service and being baptized. She told me she had a tormenting fear of audiences. I discovered she had once participated in a special church program as a child and had fainted. When she awoke, people were staring down at her. She had fallen over the communion table in front of everybody, and the fear that she might faint again in a similar situation haunted her. I discovered that the auditorium where she fainted was extremely hot, and packed with a host of people. The ventilation was poor and, being a little nervous, she probably hyperventilated. We studied this together and finally put together some facts.

Our church auditorium had a comfortable temperature, and the air conditioning was excellent. If she would relax and in loving obedience to her Lord share a witness through baptism she would not faint. When she was baptized she said, "I felt great." Her logical conclusion, plus a prayer for strength took her through this problem.

A sound mind is a fortified mind strengthened by correct information and God's Word.

As a child I was afraid of the dark. My mother paraphrased Psalm 56:3 for me. "I will trust in the Lord and not be afraid." I repeated that over and over until I fell asleep. In time, that information became my mind-set, and darkness no longer held the element of fear.

A sound mind can be reinforced with sacred music. My children were having trouble sleeping because of fear. I remembered how David sang and played his harp for the troubled King Saul. The evil spirit that discomfited him was overpowered by David's music. I thought if good music could work on that evil spirit, good music should put to flight the spirit of fear. I found the children's phonograph, put on a sacred record, and told them to hum along with it. The fear would go away, I assured them. And it did. I find that fear is always subdued within me as I begin to sing, under my breath or out loud, songs of Jesus and his love.

What can you do about your fear right now?

1. List the things you don't do and should because of debilitating fear.

2. Confess your sin of neglect and disobedience precipitated by fear.

3. Begin doing the things you need to do one at a time,

as a labor of love for God and others.

4. Plan a program of good music in life and enjoy it especially when attacked by fear.

5. Go through your Bible and underline as many verses as you can find on courage, strength, and overcoming fear. Read them often. Memorize them. Develop a sound mind.

6. Trust God to help you.

10
Loneliness

I had just been called to my first pastorate. I had just finished school, and you can imagine my unconfined joy as I preached my first sermon to my first flock, my very own flock. I was in the big league now, and this community would never be the same. The church gave me a huge two-story parsonage to live in. The house seemed a little larger after I brought in my only piece of furniture, a desk, and a few boxes of clothes. There was a knock on the door, and who should appear but a family in the church who had just visited an auction. Now I had a couple of beds and some old living room furniture. My mother had a couple of weeks to help me set up house before she flew back to Oklahoma, 1200 miles away. On the last weekend of Mother's stay my fiance came to visit us. The two favorite women of my life arranged that old house to handle the needs of an entire family.

On Monday morning, Rosene, my wife-to-be, and I took Mom to the Buffalo International Airport. As I watched her plane disappear as a speck in the sky a lump settled in my throat. Somehow, I had poorly managed to express my gratitude to her for her kindness and hard work those two weeks. Hand in hand, Rosene and I went to the car and slowly drove some miles away to the campus dorm of the college where she was in her third year of studies. After saying good-bye, I drove to my new home, about two hours away. Being quite tired, I fell asleep rather quickly.

The next day was a hard one. I kept thinking about my folks who were hundreds of miles away. It would be two years before Rosene and I would be married. Miles and time separated me from the people I loved. The anguish of spirit I experienced being cut off from those who meant so much to me was more than I could bear. That old house seemed cold and hollow, so I got in my car and drove away aimlessly. I found myself on an old road overlooking Lake Ontario. It was a cold, gray day. I stopped the car and walked down a grassy slope and sat on the edge of a bluff. The waves crashed on the rocks below. My eyes were moist. I stared into the misty horizon and poured out my grief to the Lord. Then, I heard him! Every time a wave splashed over the rocks I heard the noise of the surf say over and over to me. "I love you . . . I love you." I felt cleansed. After sitting a half-hour it seemed pointless to stay longer, so I returned to my house—this time energized and excited about what God was going to do in my life.

Loneliness is not an uncommon emotion. What a feeling it is to sit alone, knowing a special friend is with someone else! Loneliness is the ache a person feels when he is absent from work, school, or church and is not missed. It is difficult to describe the hurt one experiences when he has a problem and no one to talk with, or experiences something special and has no one to share it with. Some people live with the dread of having to eat alone. Loneliness is a special kind of grief that we feel when we're forced to be alone, but I've also seen people experience it in a crowd, even at parties.

Is loneliness something we have to live with? Aren't there situations in which loneliness will be an everyday emotion for some? Grief and loneliness are certain reactions in the event of death or separation from those we need and love, but somehow it doesn't seem a part of God's design of abundant life for us to live for prolonged periods with this overwhelming emotion. Grief and loneliness are natural, but these emotions, if prolonged, are unhealthy.

A person who wallows in loneliness, who doesn't adapt to an "alone" situation usually shows signs of self-pity. Resentment, cynicism, sarcasm, and social fear often set in. The person sometimes finds himself daydreaming and withdrawing. There's no logic to it. Loneliness triggered by the state of aloneness makes the person want to be more alone. Somehow prolonged loneliness fails to reveal any productive elements. Indeed, this emotion actually makes a person unproductive. In Psalm 42:4, David reflected on better days: "I had gone with the multitude, I went with them to the house of God, with the voice of joy and praise, with a multitude that kept holyday." But then overcome by his grief he said, "My tears have been my meat day and night. Why are thou cast down, O my soul? And why art thou disquieted within me?" (Ps. 42:3,5). Once he had been productive, a leader in spiritual things, but now he was tied up in an emotional web. It hardly seems that it is God's design for abundant living to live with prolonged loneliness.

Like other emotions, loneliness should be regarded as a

friend. It should be a reminder that the needs once fulfilled by someone special in my life are needs that can be
fulfilled in God. Loneliness is the red flag that simply
points out that I may be thinking my existence is more
dependent on others than on God. It may very well be
the evidence I needed to see that I was expecting others
to meet my needs rather than God. Loneliness may be
the persuading evidence that a somebody had become
my god and source, when Jesus wants us to understand
that he is God, that he is our Source.

A couple had moved to another state. The husband
was enjoying his work, but his wife was becoming increasingly unhappy. One night he asked his wife why she
was crying. "I miss my friends," she blurted. He felt
indignant and said, "Well, what do you think I am? Am
I not your friend? Am I not your best friend? What can
all your friends in the world give to you that I can't?"
Isn't it possible that God feels the same way when we live
with prolonged loneliness? What human being, what
creature, what friend can possibly be more to us than
God? He is the source of all need. How foolish it is for us
to live with loneliness when God wants to be all to us and
more than any living being has been.

Loneliness is our friend. It should encourage us to
enjoy the fellowship and sweet communion of Jesus as
much as we've enjoyed the companionship of someone
we've lost or have never found.

With David we should say, "O God, Thou art my
God; early will I seek thee, my soul thirsteth for thee.
Because thy loving kindness is better than life. My soul
followeth hard after thee" (Ps. 63:1, 3,8).

As guilt is the pain that drives us to confession and

repentance, loneliness is the pain that drives us to fellowship with our Lord.

How do I resolve my prolonged loneliness? Of course I must first realize that it is not God's intention for me ever to be lonely or alone. Christ said, "Behold, I stand at the door and knock; if *any man* hear my voice and open the door, I will come in to him, and will sup with him, and he with me" (Rev. 3:20, author's italics).

Lack of fellowship with him is the result of sin in my life. David said, "If I regard iniquity in my heart, the Lord will not hear me" (Ps. 66:18). If an individual has never invited Christ into his life, he will naturally struggle with the despair of loneliness. He must understand that "Christ also hath once suffered for sins, the just for the unjust, that he might bring us to God" (1 Pet. 3:18). He died so we could be brought into fellowship with him. Simply praying to receive Christ with a repentant heart will bring one into union with God.

Our church ministers to several hundred singles. Often I've seen a broken husband or wife come to know Christ in a personal way following the tragedy of divorce. The loneliness was God's way of pointing that person to a union far greater than any earthly relationship.

Christians get lonely, too. The other day I was in my office talking with an individual when the lights went out. Since my room has no windows, it was pitch black in there. If I had breathed so quietly the other person couldn't hear me, if I hadn't uttered a sound, I think that person would have begun to wonder if I were still there. Many Christians I know have let the room of their heart fill with the darkness of their bad attitudes, negativism, and sin until it is hard to discern the presence of Christ within. Loneliness results. He's there, but there's no fellowship. The answer to renewing that fellowship is to confess my sins knowing that he is willing and just to forgive and to cleanse me from all unrighteousness (1 John 1:9).

If I'm not a born again Christian I should invite Jesus into my life as my Savior and Lord to resolve my loneliness. If I'm a Christian my first step to resolving loneliness is to confess any unconfessed sin that's causing a loss of fellowship with my Lord. My self-pity, cynicism, and resentment, which so often accompany prolonged loneliness, need to be cleansed.

What should I do if I'm forced to a state of aloneness? It is important that I first understand that being alone and feeling loneliness are not the same. Jesus said, "Behold, the hour cometh, yea, is now come, that ye shall be scattered, every man to his own, and shall leave me alone: and yet I am not alone, because the Father is with me" (John 16:32). Even as Jesus had the abiding presence of the Father, so do we. Did he not say, "I will never leave thee, nor forsake thee" (Heb. 13:5).

Jean Rasmussen wrote:

> Alone with Him . . . joy is present
> and love, which says
> "alone does not mean lonely"
> for loneliness is walking the
> other way when He beckons
>   "Come".[1]

Prolonged loneliness is the result of my insistence on going my own way.

Being alone has great value. Jesus knew the importance of being alone. He would send the multitudes and his closest friends away just so he could be alone (Matt. 14:23). Moses spent time alone (Ex. 2:15; 3:1-12), as did the apostle Paul (Gal. 1:15-18; 2:1).

What should I do if I'm all alone? The following suggestions may help you to see the value of being alone.

Isaiah said, "In quietness and in confidence shall be your strength" (Isa. 30:15). Some of life's richest moments are those in which a person takes time to meditate alone. Some of the greatest dreams and aspirations have come out of meditation. The Lord promised success to Joshua (Jos. 1:8), if he would meditate on the law day and night. King David said the prosperity of a righteous man was directly related to meditation in the Word (Ps. 1). When alone, use your moments to mediate.

Jesus used alone moments for prayer (Matt. 14:23). So important were those alone moments that he actually sent people away. My wife and I treasure the times we have alone with each other just to talk. If the relationship of mates needs moments of communication, certainly time alone in conversation with God is important, too. There are times in the night that I awaken. I was once troubled because I couldn't get back to sleep, until I realized that the Lord allowed me to awaken so we could talk together. What precious conversations the Lord and I have had together in the night.

When alone we can read and write. Paul, alone in prison, asked Timothy (2 Tim. 4:13) to bring him his coat, his books, and his parchments. The Lord has brought the right books into my life at the right times. I've been amazed at how God has arranged even the order in which these books have come. Paul's reference to parchments had to do with writing materials. In our alone moments we can not only read, we can also write. Paul wrote letters to his friends, some of which are a part of the Scriptures. I know of a lady in a retirement center who writes the most beautiful letters. She's been such an encouragement to so many. A fine friend hundreds of miles away writes us the most wonderful letters, sharing poems and words of inspiration. Some have written journals that have later blessed thousands. Benjamin Franklin said that a person should write something in life of some worth or live a life worth writing about.

Our alone moments can also be filled with good music. In Ephesians 5:19, Paul spoke of making melodies in our hearts unto the Lord. When alone, we can be greatly enriched if we fill our lives with music, the Lord's music. A library of tapes and records of sacred music is a sound investment.

Vance Havner once said, "Solitude is a necessary part of Christian experience but the man who spends his time doing just that, soon has a shriveled soul not worth cultivating. Nothing develops a man's spiritual life as sharing his blessings with others. A reasonable amount of time alone is indispensable, but it is to be spent preparing him to return to the battle."[2]

God often wants us alone so he can do a great work in us. In Isaiah 40:31, we read that "they that wait upon the Lord shall renew their strength." Otherwise, we wait so we can be enabled. Moses waited forty years (Ex. 2:15; 3:1-12). Paul spent several years waiting alone in the desert before he was commissioned as an ambassador to the Gentiles (Gal. 1:15-18; 2:1). Being alone does have its advantages.

If you are "lonely," take time right now to confess the sin of not enjoying the friendship of God as much as you have the friendship of others. List areas in your life God needs to develop. Ask the Lord to begin to make these changes in your life while you're alone. Work out a strategy in which you can cooperate with God in making these changes. Being alone may become the greatest blessing of your life. Furthermore, you may learn that adjusting to aloneness and enjoying it will help you to thoroughly enjoy and live in unity with others.

Notes

1. Jean Rasmussen, *Decision Magazine*, September, 1977, © 1977 by The Billy Graham Evangelistic Association.

2. Vance Havner, *Truth for Each Day* (New Jersey: Fleming Revell, 1960).

11
How to Handle Grief

I was called to the bedside of a young lady who had taken an overdose of drugs. Only a month before she had lost her husband, who was not quite thirty. Her grief was more than she could bear.

A fine young man sat in my office and wept openly. It was a total surprise for him to learn his wife was in love with someone else. She demanded a divorce. His grief was immeasurable. A person he loved so deeply was gone. He never got his wife back, but I saw him return to a productive and eventually a grief-free life.

My best friend in high school was killed in a car accident. I was composed during the funeral, but privately I wept. The sense of loss and grief could not be contained.

Of all life's certainties death is the most certain. At some point in time everyone dies. But what about the one who walks in the valley of the shadow of death? What about the one left behind?

How do we deal with death? Is there an answer for grief? Obviously, a person can't go on indefinitely with grief in his heart. Here are some guidelines that should take the sting out of grief and shorten its duration.

Before the dread messenger summons a loved one, it is important that we have the right attitude toward those near us. I've stood by the casket of many a parent and watched children pass by to pay their last respects. Often the child who grieved the most, who required special attention and assistance at graveside, was the child who formerly treated the parent badly. The tears were tears of remorse and regret. If only that child could have had one hour with Mom or Dad alive, he could have cleared his conscience and asked forgiveness for the rebellion and disrespect.

It pays to have a clear conscience toward those close to you. When they die there is no further opportunity to clear up differences and seek reconciliation.

Second, it is important that you realize that everyone in your life belongs to God. Charles Spurgeon indicated that he had learned to hold loosely to the things of this life. That way, it wouldn't be so painful when they were taken. When we give everything to God, he gives them back not for us to own but to borrow.

When I was dating the girl who is now my wife we had reached a stage where marriage was a serious consideration. We quit dating in order to seek the mind of God regarding our futures. The separation was painful. Never had I loved anyone as I loved her. Our times were so rich, so pure. We had common spiritual goals. After we broke up I crossed the campus that dark and dreary night with an indescribable ache. During the days that followed, the Lord shared with me in his Word my need to be yielded to full-time Christian service. I didn't fight the call. On a Saturday night I woke out of a deep sleep. My mind was clear. The ache was still in my heart. God's presence was so real to me, and in those sacred moments he told me to give everything I had to him. I told him I already had, but he told me to yield anyway, and I did. A peace beyond explanation flooded my soul. I wanted to sing, and I did, under my breath, until dawn broke. Not being able to contain myself any longer, I woke my roommate and told him what happened. Later we went to church, and as we worshiped I joined zestfully in the great hymn, "When I Survey the Wondrous Cross." It was the last verse that got to me. "Were the whole ream of nature mine," if I owned the whole universe, "That were a present far too small," that wouldn't be enough to give you, Lord, for all you've done for me.

"Love so amazing, so divine, Demands my soul, my life, my all." It was then as I sang, "demands my soul, my life, my all," that suddenly, a face came to me . . . the girl I wanted to marry. "I want her, too, Ralph." I gave over the last thing I thought belonged to me. She became my Isaac! I really thought God wanted me to give her up for life. I went to see her later to break off our relationship completely and finally. Five months later the Lord returned Rosene to me. But, this time she came as a loan. In fact, our children are on loan. What possessions we have are on loan. If God should choose he can recall any of these loans. They are his. Should the day come that one of these loans is recalled, I can only praise God for the time these precious loans came under personal stewardship.

If we put claims on those close to us, not only will we suffer grief more deeply, but also anger and resentment will develop. Give your loved ones to God. They belong to him anyway.

As I write this I'm still stunned by tragic news. Only a hundred miles away the beloved pastor of a sister church and his lovely wife were shot to death in their home by burglars. What grief the two surviving teen children must be experiencing. What grief the church must share. What grief relatives and loved-ones are feeling. What do you do when grief comes?

King David had a son who died. While he was sick, "David besought God for the child, and David fasted, and went in, and lay all night upon the earth." On the seventh day the child died, and the servants were afraid to tell him. However, while they were whispering their concern, David saw them and asked, " 'Is the child dead?' And they said, 'He is dead'." Now David's response was quite unique. He got up, washed, changed his clothes, and went to the house of the Lord, where he worshiped. He then returned home and asked for a meal. While he was eating, a servant, amazed at his positive response, asked him about it. David said, "While the child was yet alive, I fasted and wept: for I said, who can tell whether God will be gracious to me that the child may live? But now he is dead, wherefore should I fast? can I bring him back again? I shall go to him, but he shall not return to me" (2 Sam. 12:15-23).

The first step in resolving his grief was attitudinal. Like Paul the apostle, he had learned the secret to stability. He accepted the death of his son. His grief would have been inordinately prolonged had he refused to accept the events as they came his way.

David reflected this attitude in his statement, "But now he is dead . . . I shall go to him, but he shall not return to me." There's a sound of finality in his statement. He realized history could not be rewritten. What had happened had happened, and it was easier in the long run for him to accept reality than to fight it. The refusal to accept the loss of a loved-one only draws out the pain and decreases days of productive living.

Second, David worshiped the Lord. This was a follow-through of his acceptance. There is no complete follow-through on the acceptance of anything in life without giving thanks to God in that which you've registered acceptance. "In every thing give thanks; for this is the will of God in Christ Jesus concerning you" (1 Thess. 5:18).

One of our high school students died following a severe concussion on the back of his head. The student body was shocked. Our high school principal called the student body together a couple of hours later in a special assembly to worship the Lord. The young man's parents were there to worship, too. Everyone had an opportunity to say, "Lord, we don't understand why but we do trust you and love you." In the atmosphere of a Christian school, 750 students were permitted an opportunity to experience healing of the wounds caused by death.

Jesus came to "bind up the brokenhearted" (Isa. 61:1). But we must approach him to allow his balm to reach our souls. "He healeth the broken in heart and bindeth up their wounds" (Ps. 147:3). So long as our hearts are in a state of rebellion and we refuse to accept God's appointed time of death, we prolong the grief. God heals those who worship, who come to him saying, "He who knows best does all things well." "My thoughts are not your thoughts, neither are your ways my ways, saith the Lord. For as the heavens are higher than the earth, so are my ways higher than your ways and my thoughts than your thoughts" (Isa. 55:8-9).

This verse was of particular help to a mother whose teenage daughter was killed in a car accident. As quickly as Job heard the tragic news of all his losses, including the death of his children, "he fell upon the ground and worshipped" (Job 1:20).

Sometimes we don't understand God's ways, but we don't have to. When a number of followers forsook Jesus because they couldn't understand him, he turned to the twelve and said, " 'Will ye also go away?' Then Simon Peter answered Him, 'Lord, to whom shall we go? thou hast the words of eternal life' " (John 6:67-68).

After the death of his child, King David also resumed his normal activities. He ate, and he returned to his responsibilities as king. Grief is prolonged if we become inactive. Satan will take advantage of those idle moments to separate us in our fellowship with God. As David's idleness led him to the sin of adultery with Bathsheba and the murder of Uriah, idleness will also lead us into negative activity. It usually starts in the mind. Grief-stricken people who become idle also become preoccupied with self. They cannot afford the self-pity which will lead them to depression and despair.

It isn't wrong to grieve. Grief is soul pain. It hurts if I'm cut by a knife. I cannot deny the real pain I feel. I cannot deny the pain of grief either. It is real. However, it is not God's purpose for me to live with prolonged grief. I must heal as quickly as possible. Much time wasted in heartache is not God's intention for me. It is not the intention of God, who said that he came to give life and that more abundantly. When I am hurt physically I don't aggravate the wound by continually reopening it. That makes no sense. Neither does it make sense to prolong grief.

The healing of grief is made possible more quickly if we accept the event causing the grief, if we worship the Lord believing that he knows best, and if we return to a busy, productive life-style.

12
Directing Desire

Often Christians are confused when they feel raging desires trying to find fulfillment. Sometimes even when we try to gain spiritual victory, these desires get the best of us, and subsequently we plunge into defeat, guilt, and depression.

What about desires? Are they wrong? Should we ask God to remove them? Sometimes these desires clamor so loudly that they appear as enemies. Actually, they should be our servants.

Christians have three basic kinds of desires. Biological desires for food, fluids, sleep, sex, rest, optimum conditions, and warmth are ever present in the Christian; so are psychological desires for success, acceptance, family, vocation, significance, and love. Special spiritual desires for God, fellowship, the Word, prayer, witnessing, and a ministry are also present in the Christian.

Desires are not to be considered good or bad. The rightness or wrongness depends upon the person's use of these desires. A river can destroy at flood time but give life if channeled for irrigation of crops. The water I drink that helps sustain life can also drown me. Desire, too, can be mastered, or it can become my master. It is my use of a desire that makes it right or wrong.

Sexual desire is a God-given desire. Some think sex is of the devil, when it was actually God who designed our bodies. The word "lust" is a biblical term describing sexual desire seeking fulfillment outside God's directives. The word "covet" is another term indicating inordinate desire.

The desire to sleep is a God-given desire. A person with proper rest is better equipped to do God's will, but excessive sleep can consume hours of productivity and usefulness. The rightness and wrongness of this desire is dependent upon control.

Psychological desires, such as the desire for success, can help thrust a person into a fruitful ministry; out of control, ambition can cause great neglect to personal health and family. I have watched people longing for success begin to spend more and more time on their vocations until they are no longer reliable as Sunday School teacher, church leaders, and witnesses. What a tragedy it is when the desire for success leads a man whose heart is not rich toward God into wealth, but what a blessing it is to see a man control and spread that desire for success in a balanced manner to family, Christian service, and vocation, enjoying success in each area.

I'm convinced that spiritual desire needs balance and control. For instance, the desire for fellowship is vital to Christian growth, but should never be exercised at the expense of Word intake, prayer, and witnessing. I've known certain spiritual eggheads who have a fantastic grasp on doctrine, but they're useless as prayer warriors and personal evangelists. Every now and then some Christians have their prayer cells but have no understanding of God's Word. A proper balance and control is necessary.

The Problem

Let's define the problem again.

Desire is wrong when it is out of control. Sex drive out of control is wrong. Sexual desire under control can be fulfilled God's way in a giving act with one's marital partner. Sexual desire is wrong when it oversteps God's designated guidelines. Desire for food is wrong when it results in gluttony. Desire for rest is wrong when it results in irresponsibility, laziness, and neglect.

Isn't it strange that the very thing that gives me problems was created by the Lord for a purpose. As a Christian, I need to consciously yield everything, even my desires, to God for him to use for his glory.

Give Your Desires to God

The path to victory over our desires is to realize they were created by Him. Thus they belong to him (Col. 1:16). Do we have a right to take what belongs to God and use it for purposes not his? (1 Cor. 6:12-20). This sobering thought should provide motivation to control our desires.

I recall a college athlete suddenly confronted with the immoral life-style of other athletes in his dorm. It was a struggle for him to remain morally pure while his friends let their desires rage uncontrollably. Finally, he talked to the Lord, saying, "God, I have hormones, too. My desires belong to you. Help me to channel them and sublimate them in ways that will bring you glory." Those hard years were victorious for this football player, because he yielded his members as instruments of righteousness.

Focus On Responsibility

To help conquer my desires, I need to focus on responsibility. For example, a young man walks into a convenience store for a carton of milk. Suddenly he's confronted with a sensual magazine cover on the counter. Desire is stimulated, and he finds it difficult to walk away. Finally, he succumbs to picking it up and buying it. *Suppose he focused on responsibility?* In his time of temptation he could ask himself, "Why am I here?" "To get a carton of milk." "What should I be doing?" "I should be en route to the milk cooler." "What is my next responsibility?" "Take the milk to the cashier and pay for it." "What next?" "Exit." By focusing on responsibility, the young man directs his energies into productive activity. The same applies to overeating. Focus on what's responsible. Say to yourself, "What should I be doing instead of eating?"

So many easily become involved in wrongly satisfying their desires because they have idle time, unplanned time, and time without purpose.

Creativity Helps

The creative person begins to think of ways to use his desires for God's glory.

A man who smokes knows that this habit is costing money and probably hurting his health. He decides to quit. His body craves tobacco. *He can translate* his urge into a reminder. Like a string around his finger, his urge can become a reminder to get involved in a positive productive activity. The after-dinner urge to smoke can be translated into "It's time for family devotions." His urge, stimulated by his friends who "light up," can be a reminder to make a positive influence on his friends, even to share a witness for Christ.

A person tempted to overeat can translate the urge into a reminder that he needs soul food from the Word and prayer.

A creative person will think of ways of channeling his drives for God's glory.

Can I Glorify God?

Often one becomes confused about whether the use of a desire is right or wrong. The question one could ask is, "Does this glorify God?"

Once my father was asked by a young mother how to quit smoking. He promptly replied, "When you get that cigarette out simply say, 'I light this in the name of Jesus and smoke it for the glory of God.' " It is amazing how clearly right or wrong something is when you think of it in this manner.

Spirit Empowered

There is no substitute for God's power. The power of the cross can give control and direction. We can realize a supernatural strength beyond ourselves. Such strength is ours when we wait on the Lord (Isa. 40:30) and rejoice in all things (Neh. 8:10).

I have known of people who instantly overcame their

desires because God miraculously provided a life-time cure. God is still God!

The Spirit-filled life is the life that will evidence special fruit. Paul tells us that one of the fruits is "discipline." Let God be God by controlling your desires.

13
Power in Peace

What is peace? Is it tranquillity? Is it solitude or a moment of quietness? Is it inner security? Is it cessation of conflict? Perhaps all of these describe peace. Without a doubt, peace is the desire of every human heart.

For years I lived with the torment of not knowing a personal relationship with God through Jesus Christ. The night I trusted him as my Savior a peace came to my heart and mind.

How does one acquire peace? We try everything from manipulating circumstances to taking pills. Obviously, neither works. Manipulation is as futile as trying to change the direction of wind. Tranquilizers have a very temporary effect.

The Holy Spirit and Peace

Peace is the result of a Spirit-filled life. In Galatians 5:22, the fruit of the Spirit is "love, joy, peace." "To be spiritually minded is life and peace," Paul reminded the Romans (8:6). He also referred to peace in the Holy Ghost in Romans 14:17 and to the fact that peace came by the power of the Holy Ghost in Romans 15:13.

We are filled by the Holy Spirit by faith in his promise that "if we ask anything according to His will, He hears us" (1 John 5:14-15). What is his will? In Ephesians 5:18,

113

we read, "be filled with the [Holy] Spirit." Of course, that's a command, but if a command, then certainly his will.

To be filled with his Holy Spirit I must first be empty of impurity. On the basis of 1 John 1:9, my sin can be dealt with through sincere confession and acceptance of his forgiveness. As I yield myself to his gracious control, the Holy Spirit fills me by faith. Perhaps the most significant step to acquiring peace would be to make a list of unconfessed sins and apply 1 John 1:9 to your list.

My wife and I were invited to a Christian resort in the verdant Adirondack Mountains. One night we enjoyed the testimony of a layman, who shared the dynamic power of being filled with the Spirit. As a pastor, I had all the doctrine, but lacked the full knowledge of this kind of walk with the Lord. I eagerly listened. In the first session we were asked to write out a "sin list" of all unforgiven sins. When time was up I was still writing. Everyone else seemed to be finished. I went to our room and remarked to my wife on the futility of this exercise. There were certainly more sins to confess. Into the night I continued to confess.

At the next session it was pointed out that forgiveness was realized as we agreed with the Holy Spirit's conviction of sin in our lives. I then realized that I had been playing Holy Spirit. I was doing all the convicting. Then I saw a word in 1 John 1:9, that brought a new kind of light to my life. "If we confess our sins, he is faithful and just to forgive us our sins, and to cleanse us from all unrighteousness." The word was "all!" It occurred to me that I didn't have to remember all my sins, only agree with the Holy Spirit about the sins he pointed out, and then he would cleanse me from *all* unrighteousness, even the sins I couldn't remember, even the sins I committed ignorantly. I sat right back and enjoyed forgiveness and cleansing. There I was, a cleansed, perfectly clean vessel.

In those next moments I appropriated the fullness of the Holy Spirit by faith. I can't say I felt different, and there weren't any immediate evidences of being filled! But what happened in the next months was gratifying. I was able, by his Spirit, to lead more people to Christ during the next two months than I had in the previous five years of of my ministry.

Peace is the result of Spirit-filled living, and this I can attest to by the experience of over twelve years.

Reconciliation and Peace

The word "peace" in the original language carries with it the idea of reconciliation. In otherwords, my inner peace is contingent on whether I have peace with others. The first relationship I need to resolve is my relationship to God. Is Christ my Savior? Is he my Lord? Is there anything between the Lord Jesus and me that needs to be removed? "Therefore being justified by faith, we have peace with God through our Lord Jesus Christ" (Rom. 5:1).

Second, I will find peace when I resolve relationships in which *I've offended others.* It's important to clear one's conscience. Not to do so is to carry a debt. If I steal I make restitution, and if I've offended I ask forgiveness.

George was a gruff man. He once shot someone in self-defense, and once pulled the trigger on a deputy sheriff, but the gun wouldn't go off. Through my father, the Lord touched the life of this man, and he was gloriously

saved. Then George did something that I'll never forget.
He took three weeks off from work, and each working
day he backed up to his garage and filled his trailer with
items he had stolen. How he remembered where each
came from is difficult for me to understand. But he returned everything. What peace he experienced as he
made it right with people he had wronged!

As we observe the Lord's Supper in our church it's
become customary for us to pause for a few minutes of
silence while we examine ourselves before partaking.
What a sight! Children cross the aisles to find their parents, teens look for their friends, couples and families
walk to the front to huddle in prayer at the altar, and it's
not uncommon to see someone exit to locate the nearest
phone. Why? To prepare themselves adequately for this
ordinance church members are aware that barriers have
to be removed. There is no peace like that which comes
from settling accounts with others.

Third, I will find peace when I resolve relationships in
which *others have offended me.* Matthew 18:15-17
makes it clear that I should go to the brother who has
offended me, tactfully and lovingly repair things, and
win my brother. I should go to great lengths to make sure
such relationships are healed. Peace comes from resolving relationships. I realize this is unpopular. In fact, it's a
new concept to many Christians. It seems easier to
approach someone I've offended and ask forgiveness
than to approach someone who's offended me. Do I just
walk up to someone and say "Ah, I want to talk to you,
ah—you see, you offended me." This old principle is
rarely practiced, and for some it's unknown. I would like
to treat this subject especially as it relates to peace.

Why can't I just forgive a person who has hurt me and let it go at that? Why should I go to someone who's offended me? Isn't that like saying, "Please feel sorry for me, I'm hurt?"

Let me suggest some good reasons for approaching your brother who's offended you.

In the first place, it's a unique opportunity to point out to a brother that what he may consider an acceptable trait is really a fault and a grievous hindrance to fellowship with others. A man may take pride in his forthrightness and outspoken ways. If enough people approach him who've been offended by his manner, he may see that his ways are not a sign of courage but a sign of callousness and stupidity.

Second, the Bible says "if [your brother] be overtaken in a fault, ye which are spiritual restore such a one in the spirit of meekness; considering thyself, lest thou also be tempted" (Gal. 6:1). Moreover, going to my brother who's offended me gives me an opportunity to build him up, sometimes restore him, and help him in his time of need. A man once struck me in the face. Of course, I didn't hit him back. His outburst erupted from a broken heart. I stayed by him. Days later he said he and the Lord had everything patched up. My approach was to help, to restore, to heal. The offense was not the issue. The issue was a hurt and broken man.

Let me share a word of caution. Don't approach your brother about his offense without first determining what offended you. Irreparable damage can be dealt a man if he's approached and the reason for the meeting isn't known.

One afternoon a friend stopped by our home. He was

troubled. Earlier that day a fine, sincere church member walked up to my friend and said, "For some reason I don't understand, I've resented you, and I'm asking you to forgive me." He never stated what the offense was. Only two weeks earlier another church member came to my friend asking forgiveness for the same reason. The fact that neither church member specified what it was about my friend that evoked resentment caused him to seek out through prayer and counsel the ways he was being offensive.

When we approach someone who's offended us, we should indicate what the offense is so the brother can correct it and grow spiritually. This whole principle is a selfless, loving, and edifying act.

An offense should be cleared lovingly, considerately, diplomatically, and cautiously. The objective is to "win" the brother. It should be done privately and confidentially. The Bible indicates that the brother could respond negatively towards overtures of reconciliation, and that's when the offended person should then take along another "healer" or restorer. The objective is not to "have it out" but to mend.

This principle can be practiced at home, where offenses may be quite frequent. As children learn the principle, they'll use it elsewhere. Adults, too, will find the home environment an excellent place to school themselves in carrying out this principle. The result? Peace.

I think the reason my wife and I have a relationship so free of tension and in which we thoroughly enjoy each other is because we frankly share with each other what's offensive and what's acceptable.

If we can approach our brother and praise him for

doing what's acceptable, why can't we approach him when he's been offensive? If he'll listen the positive results will be amazing. Incidently, it's not a bad idea to find your brother at a later date after clearing the offense and reinforce your relationship with a word of praise or act of kindness.

Peace is the result of mending relationships. Indeed the word *peace* carries with it the idea of reconciliation.

Behavior and Peace

In Psalm 37:11, 37 we find that the meek, righteous, and upright experience peace. Right behavior produces peace.

The day should begin with activity that will bring peace. The best activity is involvement with God's Word. Psalm 119:165 says, "Great peace have they who love thy law." Concentration on the Lord during one's quiet time in the Word unquestionably brings peace. "Thou wilt keep him in perfect peace, whose mind is stayed on thee" (Isa. 26:3).

As the day continues, right behavior will be followed by peace. Wrong behavior will prompt inner conflict. "There is no peace, saith my God, to the wicked" (Isa. 57:21).

Prayer and Peace

Paul said, "Be careful for nothing; but in every thing by prayer and supplication with thanksgiving let your requests be made known unto God. And the peace of God which passeth all understanding shall keep your hearts and minds through Christ Jesus" (Phil. 4:6-7).

Prayer plus thanksgiving equals peace. There is no

substitute for praise in an effort to acquire peace.

The hurricane is destructive. The swirling mass of air with its raging winds puts in peril everything in its path. But at the very center of the hurricane, the eye, there's a remarkable calm. Just like the Christian! At the center of his life should be a calm, an unexplainable peace. Life is much more enjoyable with peace, even if everything's falling apart. And that peace is the result of the fervent prayer of a righteous man who offers praise with his prayer.

14
Learning to Love

In college I associated quite frequently with an upper-classman at the radio station. He was an obnoxious type who bragged often. I tried to avoid him, but there were times when we had to work together. I learned to thoroughly dislike him. His repulsive style was too much for me to handle. Finally, taking the matter to the Lord in prayer, I found some answers and later became about the closest friend this obnoxious guy had. How do you learn to love someone you loathe?

We often pray for love, and it doesn't come. We admire people who do love and wish we could be just like them. "If only I had the capacity to love like he does," we say.

For openers, I would suggest that real love is not necessarily a feeling but a process of doing. Feeling is a by-product of loving.

Jesus never described love in terms of feeling but always in terms of action. "A new commandment I give unto you, That ye love one another," he told his disciples (John 13:34). John said we should love "in deed" (1 John 3:18). Note the action words of Matthew 5:44, "love . . . bless . . . do good to . . . pray for." Paul said, "Bear ye one another's burdens, and so fulfil the law of Christ" (Gal. 6:2).

Loving Others Is Our Way of Loving God

God has provided some unique incentives for showing love toward people we don't like. For instance, in Matthew 25:40 he said, "Inasmuch as you have done it unto the least of these my brethren, you have done it unto me." In Luke 6:32-35 Jesus points out that it's easy to love someone who is lovable and suggests that a test of real love is to love someone who is unlovable. I once recall wishing that I could truly love God with all my heart, mind, and strength. It was then that the Lord pointed out to me that I could get started by loving others. Loving others, especially the least of the brethren, indeed the unlovely, is a unique way to love God.

The love of God responds to need no matter who has the need. Human love usually responds to the need of someone who will appreciate the gesture of kindness, whereas divine love will demonstrate itself toward someone who may not appreciate the act of love as well as to those who will appreciate it.

Let's consider two children. One is starving and bears all the marks of emaciation, tummy protruding, etc. He's so weak he can't cry. The other child hasn't had food in two or three days, but he's on the pudgy side and behaves insolently. He is angrily demanding food. Now, which child would you respond to sooner? Human love moves toward the pitiful. Divine love moves toward the need. The attitude of the recipient has nothing to do with the demonstration of love.

Feelings Are By-products of Love

Many psychologists after Guthrie say, "Feelings follow

behaviour." C. S. Lewis made a classic statement in his book *Mere Christianity* when he said, "Do not try to manufacture feelings; ask yourself, if I were sure that I loved, what would I do? And when you have found the answer, go do it. He will give us feelings of love as He pleases."[1]

As one person put it, "My experience has been that if I begin acting in love the feeling of love may follow."

Again, love is always scripturally described in terms of doing, not feeling. The feeling is not so important as the act, but so often feelings of love become the by-product of selfless acts.

How Did Jesus' Love Feel?

If we could have asked Jesus in the garden the night before the crucifixion, "Jesus, how does love feel?" I think he would have answered, "Agonizing." If someone had asked Jesus on the cross, "How does love feel right now?" I think his answer would have been, "Painful."

Love Is in Every Christian

Where do we get love? Romans 5:5 says that it comes from the Holy Spirit. "The love of God is shed abroad in our hearts by the Holy [Spirit]." Galatians 5:22 states that love is a fruit of the Spirit. This dynamic finds its source in God. First John 4:8 says that God is love. John 14:1-10 says that Jesus is God. Therefore, Jesus is love. John 1:12 says that "as many as received him [Jesus] . . . became the sons of God." If I'm God's child, I have Jesus in my heart and, therefore, have love.

When we look at some dynamic Christian and say to

ourselves, "I wish I had the love he does," we must realize that he has no more love than any other believer. We are all indwelt by God who is love. The problem is not getting love but getting it out.

A businessman had learned some of these truths and had an opportunity to test them. At a convention he was in a receiving line with some colleagues, shaking hands with the guests that passed by. When a little freckle-faced boy, with his parents, shook hands, the business-man asked the little fellow his name. When the man repeated it, he accidentally mispronounced it. The little guy turned up his face and called him a really crude name. As the line passed on, the insulted boy kept turn-ing back screaming out this disgusting name. The busi-nessman was really embarrassed. As president of his company he had looked forward to this trip as being profitable. He hadn't counted on this episode. Every-where he went in the next two days he ran into this kid and was always greeted with the same ugly name. In his attempt to avoid these confrontations he sneaked around back passageways, even through the kitchen.

One morning in his quiet time he prayed that God would love through him. When he stepped into the ele-vator he saw his freckle-faced foe, alone. All kinds of thoughts ran through his head as he looked down at his traveling companion. Then he prayed quietly, "Lord, help me love." Something unusual happened. The little fellow looked up at him, their eyes met, and suddenly he wanted to take that little guy in his arms and hug him. His prayer was answered, and his foe became his buddy. It all began when he decided to love.

How do I release love? By faith. Here is a simple but

effective exercise. Picture in your mind a person you can't love and repeat this fact, "God loves you." Remember Christ died for him, that person you hate! *Second,* say, "Jesus in me loves you." Keep saying that until you understand that the most important part of you loves that person you loathe. *Third,* say, "I love you." Say it until you mean it. You may have to start all over again. It won't hurt. Listen to yourself make these statements.

How do I release love? If the person you think you can't love were your best friend, think what you would do for him. List those things. Now, after listing these, begin to do them one at a time. God will bless your action, and who knows, you may begin to feel feelings of love!

Oscar Hammerstein reportedly wrote these words to Mary Martin before she went on stage in a production:

> A bell is no bell till you ring it,
> A song is no song till you sing it,
> Love in your heart wasn't put there to stay.
> Love isn't love till you give it away.[2]

Go love by faith and let the feelings come when they may.

Notes

1. C.S. Lewis, *Mere Christianity* (New Jersey: Macmillan, 1952), p. 102.

2. Oscar Hammerstein, "Sixteen Going on Seventeen," *The Sound of Music* (New York: Williamson Music Co., 1959).

15
Joy

The fruit of the Holy Spirit is joy. Joy should be evident in every Christian, but unfortunately it isn't.

How well I remember preaching on the joy of salvation as a young preacher. "Find Christ and you'll experience joy," I would declare. Then in my office, I would pray, "Lord, I feel so hypocritical. I tell people if they'll find a new relationship with Christ they'll have joy. I have Christ, but I have no joy."

Most people think that joy comes when everything goes right. The only joy they realize is when the arrangement of circumstances is perfect. Do you realize how rarely that magic moment takes place?

The word "blessed" in the Beatitudes is the King James Version's translation of the Greek word *makarios*. Cyprus was named by the Greeks *he makaria* which means "the happy isle." Cyprus was so lovely, rich, and fertile, that a man would never need to go beyond its coastline to find the perfectly happy life. The word *happiness* contains the root word *hap* which means "chance." For centuries man has looked for the moment when all would be just right to enjoy his capsule of joy.

How many times in life is everything "just right"? Joy dependent upon the arrangement of circumstances is rare and fleeting.

Divine joy, however, is not dependent upon the arrangement of circumstances. This is what Christ spoke of when he said "that my joy might remain in you, and that your joy might be full" (John 15:11).

The source of real joy is God, and this joy is made possible to us through the ever abiding presence of the Holy Ghost in the believer. In Romans 14:17 Paul said the "kingdom of God is not meat and drink but . . . joy in the Holy Ghost." And where is the kingdom of God? Jesus said "the kingdom of God is within you" (Luke 17:21). According to 1 Corinthians 6:19, the Spirit of God makes the believer's body his temple. Since the fruit of the Holy Spirit is love, joy, and peace, we must conclude that if joy is in the Holy Ghost and the Holy Ghost is in the believer, then the believer has joy!

If you are a Christian you have joy in you, whether you feel it or not. "But, if joy is in me then why don't I experience it?"

Let's picture a piano in a room. A hymnal is on it. I may see the piano and I may see the hymnal, but I hear no music. Before I hear any music, it is obvious that the notes and instrument must be activated. Joy must be activated, too. But, how is it activated?

Joy is activated by faith when we begin to rejoice. We rejoice not by feelings but by faith.

What is our basis for rejoicing and thanking God in life's every situation? Romans 8:28 says that "all things work together for good to them that love God, who are the called according to his purpose." That's why Paul said, "Rejoice evermore" and "In every thing give thanks: for this is the will of God in Christ Jesus concerning you" (1 Thess. 5:16,18).

A destitute rancher in California sold his ranch to join the gold rush. The new owner, Colonel Sutter, had a small daughter who, while playing, brought the colonel some yellow "marbles." He later discovered they were gold. Later he unearthed more gold, $38,000,000 worth! The destitute rancher had it all the time but didn't know it.

You, believer, have joy within you. Discover it! Don't run off to everything that says "joy is here." Take advantage of your inner resource and activate it by faith. Rejoice!

Joy has an opportunity to be most evident in hard times. They say that little birds in the Florida Everglades sing their loudest and best when the nights are darkest and stormiest. Just so the Christian.

Now, let's make it a little easier. To rejoice is simple compliance to a scriptural command. In Matthew 5:12 it says, "Rejoice, and be exceeding glad." Paul says it two different ways in 1 Thessalonians 5:16,18, when he reminds us to "Rejoice evermore" and in "In every thing give thanks." Now, we know the Bible says a great deal about loving others, but did you know that in the New Testament alone we are called upon to rejoice seventy times?

In 1 Peter 4:13, we are exhorted to rejoice in times of suffering and sickness. E. Stanley Jones once said, "Don't bear pain, use it. Turn it into a testimony!"[1]

In Madagascar, Christians hiding in caves asked to sing. Their leader implored them not to or their location would be given away. So, they sang under their breath. These same Christians were later found and hurled over the cliffs to certain death, but it was reported that this time they were singing full voice.

A Korean pastor and his family chose to be killed for their faith rather than deny the Christ they loved. They were buried alive. As the dirt was thrown on top of them, the children began singing. As the dirt covered everything but their heads they still sang. They could hardly breathe from the pressure on their lungs. Their little faces turned black as sweet melodies were still on their lips. Nearly everyone who watched became Christians, and many of them are still alive today, serving the Lord.

When did Habakkuk rejoice? "Although the fig tree shall not blossom, neither shall fruit be in the vines; the labour of the olive shall fail, and the fields shall yield no meat; the flock shall be cut off from the fold, and there shall be no herd in the stalls: Yet, I will rejoice in the Lord, I will joy in the God of my salvation" (Hab. 3:17-18).

About six years ago the Lord called my wife and me into a ministry to families. In addition to a counseling practice, I traveled around the country holding seminars in local churches on family life and what the Scriptures say about it. We were not supported by any group, just operated by faith. What an experience! We bumped into some genuine character building times, I'll assure you.

At one point, we reached a very low period financially, and the going was rough. I worked diligently, but everything went bone dry. I rode my bicycle to the office, since we had no money for extra gas. One Saturday night after the children were in bed, I looked at my wife across the living room and saw a tear course down her face. Now that hurt. I was the breadwinner, and it seemed that somehow I had failed to let God provide through me. My family was suffering, and I didn't enjoy it. "I know this sounds silly," she said, "but do you ever get the idea that God's forgotten us?" I tried to comfort, "But the Bible says that God is not unjust to forget our labor of love. God will certainly provide." We had rationed enough gas to drive to church and back Sunday morning. We certainly enjoyed the time of worship and fellowship.

On the way home we drove about two blocks, and the car chugged to a stop. There we were, a dime in my wife's pocketbook and sixty-seven cents in the checkbook. We had eaten everything in the house. I don't know how she had made the meals look so good the past few days but she had. And just before we had run out of gas Rosene announced that there was nothing to eat in the house unless we had some money to stop and buy a few groceries. That's when we discovered the sum total of seventy-seven cents.

Well, there we sat in the parking lot by the side of the street. We just quietly huddled as a family, my six-year-old son, four-year-old daughter, and wife. We put our arms around each other and prayed, "Lord, we don't understand why we're in this situation but have learned that it's in times like this that you desire to prove yourself strong. So, we thank you for this circumstance and now ask you to provide a miracle or some wisdom to help us out. In Jesus' name we pray, amen."

I took the dime and crossed the street to a pay phone to call the church we attended to see if one of the members who had a gas station down the street would lend us some fuel. He wasn't there, but when one of the ministers who answered heard we were out of gas, he laughed, thinking it was hilarious, and said he'd come down and help us. I didn't even have time to explain I had no money, and knowing him, I thought he probably didn't have any either.

Later he drove up. I was trying to figure out how to tell him I was out of money. Before I could he walked over, opened up his hand and offered me three five-dollar-bills. He said, "Somebody told me he owed you this." I didn't remember anyone owing me anything but eagerly received the payment. "Wow, honey, look at this." It seemed like a million dollars. That got us home and helped us buy groceries.

Tuesday arrived, and we were dry again. However, as we opened the mail, a $50 check fell out of one envelope and a $600 check was enclosed in the next. It was worth it to rejoice when the going was rough. Days later we received another check for our ministry, this time for $30,000!

God fulfilled his promise to us when he said in 2 Corinthians 9:8, "And God is able to make all grace abound toward you; that ye, always having all sufficiency in all things, may abound to every good work."

It's time to rejoice. Rejoice in everything now. You'll do it later when it turns out for the good. So, why not do it now by faith and savor the joy God wants you to experience?

When things are at their worst is when God wants you to have joy the most. And it is yours as you rejoice by faith.

Note

1. E. Stanley Jones, *Song of Ascents*

Appendix
How to Know Christ
Personally

Have you ever made the wonderful discovery of knowing Jesus in a personal way for yourself, or would you say you are still in the process? If you haven't, and desire to know him personally, to be guaranteed of eternal life, and to be able to start life anew, you will find the following information helpful.

Physical laws, such as the law of gravity, do not change. Even if you don't like them or try to ignore them, they are still in operation. Likewise, God has some spiritual laws which are in effect whether we like or dislike them. I want to show you four of these principles.

1. GOD LOVES YOU AND WANTS TO GIVE YOU AN ABUNDANT AND ETERNAL LIFE. John 10:10: "The thief cometh not, but for to steal, and to kill, and to destroy: I am come that they might have life, and that they might have it more abundantly."
John 3:16: "For God so loved the world, that he gave his only begotten Son, that whosoever believeth in him should not perish, but have everlasting life."

II. BUT MAN IS SINFUL AND SEPARATED FROM GOD AND THE LIFE GOD OFFERS. Romans 3:23: "For all have sinned, and come short of the glory of God."
Romans 6:23: "For the wages of sin is death; but the gift of God is eternal life through Jesus Christ our Lord."

This diagram will help to illustrate:

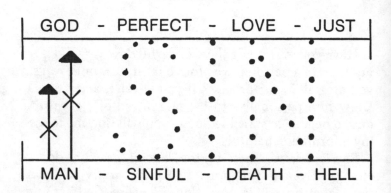

Note that it is our sin that separates us from God. I want to show you how to come to God. But first let me emphasize that you cannot come to God by "going to church" or "turning over a new leaf." That's why the arrows have an "X" through them. They represent our attempts to get to God.

III. JESUS CHRIST IS GOD'S ONLY PROVISION FOR MAN'S SIN. THROUGH HIM YOU CAN COME TO GOD AND HAVE THE LIFE GOD OFFERS.

Note the word "only." This is because of what Jesus says in John 14:6: "I am the way, the truth, and the life:

no man cometh unto the Father, but by me." 1 Peter 3:18 explains why Jesus made this statement. ("For Christ also hath once suffered for sins, the just for the unjust, that he might bring us to God, being put to death in the flesh, but quickened by the Spirit.") A cross on the diagram shows that while we can't get to God by our efforts, God will come to us.

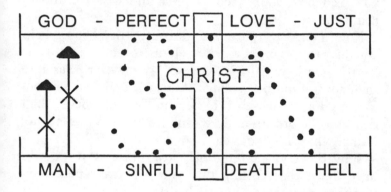

Believing all of this, however, does not make you a Christian.

IV. YOU MUST RECEIVE CHRIST IN FAITH BY PERSONAL INVITATION.

John 1:12 emphasizes that we must *receive* Christ: "But as many as received him, to them gave he power to become the sons of God, even to them that believe on his name."

Revelation 3:20 tells what it means to receive: "Behold, I stand at the door, and knock: if any man hear my voice, and open the door, I will come in to him, and will sup with him, and he with me."

Occasionally when I ask someone if he would like to ask Christ into his heart, he says he doesn't "feel" like it. Fortunately the Bible does not say an emotional "feeling" is necessary. It says "Whosoever will, let him take the water of life freely" (Rev. 22:17). The issue is whether you recognize your need of Jesus and will ask him to come in.

Now, I can't pray for you, of course. But I could help you to pray a prayer asking Jesus to come into your heart. Matthew 10:32-33 says, "Whosoever therefore shall confess me before men, him will I confess also before my Father which is in heaven. But whosoever shall deny me before men, him will I also deny before my Father which is in heaven."

Why don't you let me help you pray? And we will have the understanding that you will not repeat anything you don't mean in your heart.

Prayer: "Dear God, I know I have sinned. I have done many things wrong. But I know you love me. And I know you sent Jesus to die for me. I believe Christ rose from the dead and lives today. I know he said he would come into my heart if I asked him. So Jesus, I ask you to come in right now. Save me—cleanse me—forgive me—and be the Lord of my life. I put my faith in you right now and thank you for saving me. Amen."

Now Christ said he would come in if you asked him. You have asked him—so where is he right now?

Why don't you take the opportunity to pray a prayer of thanksgiving right now? Be sure to call a Bible-believing, Christ-honoring pastor and ask him to help you with the next steps in your walk with the Lord. Confess your new faith through baptism and become part of a fellowship of believers that will nurture you.